H♥PE STORIES

First published in 2020.

ISBN: 978-1-86922-864-4 (Printed)
ISBN: 978-1-86922-865-1 (ePDF)

Published by KR Publishing
P O Box 3954
Randburg
2125
Republic of South Africa

Tel: (011) 706-6009
Fax: (011) 706-1127
E-mail: orders@knowres.co.za
Website: www.kr.co.za

Typesetting, layout and design: Cia Joubert, cia@knowres.co.za
Cover design: Adele Wallace, adele@cwdi.co.za
Copywriters and Editing: Cassidy Parker & Robyn Maclarty
Proofreading: KR Team, krpublishing@knowres.co.za
Project management: Cia Joubert, cia@knowres.co.za

H♥PE STORIES

LET HOPE BE YOUR STRENGTH

27 STORIES OF COURAGE & INSPIRATION IN UNPRECEDENTED TIMES

by

Lesley Waterkeyn,
Sandy Van Dijk &
Dawn Nathan-Jones

kr
publishing

2020

ACKNOWLEDGEMENTS

Thank you to all our contributors who took the time to tell us their stories and remind us that there is always hope.

We'd also like to thank Cassidy Parker, Robyn Maclarty and Simone Isaacs for their attention to detail and their assistance in putting this book together.

Thank you to our friend Julia Finnis-Bedford for inviting us to do the 21-day abundance meditation to renew a sense of trust and optimism about our life and our world, which inspired *Hope Stories*. Thank you to Adele Wallace for the incredible cover design. We would like to extend our appreciation and gratitude towards CWDi for their creative expertise as well as The Lime Envelope for your hard work and dedication in realising our goal with this book.

And finally, thank you to our families for believing in us and putting up with the endless hours of Zoom interviews during the hard lockdown on level 5.

MESSAGE OF HOPE FROM PROF. THULI MADONSELA

Thank you for giving people HOPE through this book. Hope is what people need most in times of radical uncertainty or change. The stories are heart warming and hope inspiring. I particularly like the fact that it is an easy read that can be read over and over.

It is an honour to be included in your remarkable book.

"Hope is the little spark that gives you faith in the possibility of a future that seems unattainable. If you lose hope, you lose everything"

– Prof Thuli Madonsela

TABLE OF CONTENTS

ABOUT US

Over the Rainbow (OTR) is a social enterprise that aims to strengthen and extend entrepreneurship ecosystems by providing entrepreneurs with the knowledge connections and support that will enhance their success in business.

Our organization is led by entrepreneurial woman, who strongly believe that the greatest way to "action against poverty" is by upskilling entrepreneurs so that they are able to build and lead sustainable, scalable businesses that will in turn employ other people. Our entrepreneurship training follows the colours of the rainbow and serves to move the entrepreneur's business ideas and concepts to the next stage of growth.

As well as providing a platform to grow, develop and showcase their business, our training promotes networking and collaborating.

To date, OTR have trained over 5000 entrepreneurs at various venues around South Africa and in partnership with some key organisations who are driven to make an impact and difference to entrepreneurs and communities in our country.

Lesley Waterkeyn

Message of Hope:

"In hope, I am fearless."

The founder and vice chairman of CWDi, Lesley Waterkeyn is a natural rainmaker whose generous and infectious entrepreneurial spirit uplifts and inspires others to do more than they imagined possible. Lesley has steered the transformation of Colourworks from a small print agency to a fully integrated marketing agency specialising in strategic brand experiences. Colourworks was founded in 1998. The company has an impressive client base and deals with blue-chip companies throughout South Africa.

A lifelong learner and active member of the world's largest peer-to-peer entrepreneurial network, Entrepreneurs' Organisation (EO), Lesley is passionate about unlocking the potential of South Africa's young people. Amongst many other accolades, Lesley is a multiple award-winning entrepreneur.

Lesley is married to Mark and has three boys, including a set of twins. She is one of four sisters, with two of her sisters working with her. She is a keen runner and ran the New York marathon in 2017. She believes that staying fit and healthy are critical to ensuring she has the energy to continue to build her businesses and influence others to live their best lives.

Sandy Van Dijk

Message of Hope:

"Bond with others to give them hope."

Sandy spent more than 25 years in the classroom inspiring her students to be the best they could be and giving of herself.

In 2014, while on a book writing experience, she met NY bestselling authors of the book The Passion Test, Janet Bray and Chris Attwood. Through doing the Passion Test herself, she decided to become a facilitator and help others find their purpose and destiny. Sandy has reignited her love of teaching and gets to live her passion through sharing this Passion Test process.

Today, Sandy is COO of Over the Rainbow, a social enterprise dedicated to empowering entrepreneurs. Founded with her sister, Lesley they have written a book called The Entrepreneurs Playbook which follows the colors of the rainbow. The book aims to inspire entrepreneurs by changing their 'what if's into how to's,' sustain their businesses and achieve success. She is married and has 2 grown-up children.

Dawn Nathan-Jones

Message of Hope:

"Challenges are opportunities that life gives us so we can become the best version of ourselves, they release the greatness, hope and power that lies in all of us."

Dawn Nathan-Jones is a renowned South African entrepreneur, multiple award-winning business leader and a professional speaker. Her legacy lies in her role as one of the early pioneers of the Imperial Car Rental company, known more recently as Europcar. She spent over three decades building this fledging car rental business with her two colleagues. At the end of her illustrious career as CEO, she stepped down and in 2016, launched into reality TV with her role as the only female Shark in the M-Net reality show, Shark Tank South Africa.

Dawn's trajectory has taken a more holistic and intentional direction that focuses on spending time with her family in Cape Town, and giving back to communities. Part of giving back involves developing strategic partnerships with the aim to aid fledging businesses, specifically focused on youth and women. One of these partnerships is her investment in Over the Rainbow, a social enterprise NPO that strengthens entrepreneurship ecosystems by providing entrepreneurs with resources that will enhance their success and sustainability in business. Dawn's passion for female and youth development not only stems from her role as a successful businesswoman, but from her succinct ability to understand the difficulties women face in starting their own businesses. Dawn is a single mother to her son Daniel.

OUR STORY

OVER THE RAINBOW
by Les, Sandy and Dawn

"Let hope be your strength."

A Relentless Hope

Back in 2015, we remember our business community and fellow entrepreneurs being in full strategy mode. At the time, we were all developing five-year plans, and most of us were predicting light at the end of what had been a long and tough tunnel. The aftermath of the global financial crisis in 2008, consistent bouts of political uncertainty, a weakening rand, an energy resource crisis, drought, corruption, crime and many other issues had been hampering the economy for years. But we shared a relentless hope that, by 2020, these issues would be a thing of the past.

And when it finally came, it certainly seemed that 2020 was going to be our year. We'd spent the five years prior doing our research, writing our first book and training over 2,000 entrepreneurs. Since then, we'd launched our book on an online learning platform, landed our biggest deal ever, and accepted the opening slot at eight I AM AN ENTREPRENEUR summits with Andile Khumalo. There was no doubting it: we were on our way to the next big thing.

One of the First Cases in the Western Cape

In early February 2020, we had an Over the Rainbow partners meeting at the Vineyard Hotel in Cape Town. The opportunities we'd mapped out to enhance our business model were taking shape, our diaries were starting to fill up with small and large entrepreneur workshops and conferences, and Dawn had talks with a number of big corporates lined up. This was our year to empower entrepreneurs and make a difference, we just knew it!

On the morning of Thursday, 12 March, Dawn attended a meeting with a very talented fashion entrepreneur who had secured additional investment to expand her business into wider markets. She was sharing her impressive vision for the year, when she decided to check her persistently beeping phone. She found four messages from her son, Daniel: "Mom, please come and fetch me, the school has the coronavirus!"

She paid, left and rushed to Daniel's school to find a load of anxious and confused kids waiting for their parents outside the gate. One of the children's fathers had tested positive for Covid-19 – one of the first cases in the Western Cape – and the principal had made the courageous decision to temporarily close the school. Learners, teachers and parents were worried. At the time, Covid-19 still seemed confined to China, Europe, the UK and the USA, but the sense that we were relatively safe was starting to unravel.

The Coughing Companion

Despite these developments, the working world was still mostly operating as usual and we had 15 flights booked for our team to deliver our Passion Test and Over the Rainbow training programme at various summits around the country. The first was in Johannesburg on 14 March, and our excitement was tangible. We couldn't wait to positively influence the more than 200 entrepreneurs we were about to meet. We were not deterred by murmurs of the virus – we posed in front of a banner that said in big letters, "Be fearless!", and we carried on. This wasn't going to affect us.

On the plane back to Cape Town later that afternoon, Sandy and Les sat in their allocated seats – 3A and 3B, where Les likes to sit, right up front. (She always tells her children that if you sit in the front, you get there first.) We settled in for our two-hour flight and started discussing what we felt had been a successful day. We talked through what we had learnt and how we could implement these lessons at the seven summits that were still on our horizon, including what we could improve and what we could do differently.

A moment later, the gentleman sitting next to Sandy started coughing – not just a slight cough but a really serious cough. We were a little unnerved and the close confines of the aeroplane suddenly became all that more obvious. Les reached into her handbag for some tissues so that we could cover our faces and we shared some hand sanitiser. Within seconds, Covid-19 felt closer than it had ever been before. Although we didn't catch Covid-19 from our friend on the plane, the world was days away from the greatest shift anyone had seen in several generations.

Closer and Closer

During the weeks that followed, more rumours, reports and conspiracy theories started circling. Les remembers her son saying to her, "Mom, I bet you (he likes to bet) that we will know someone who has Covid-19 within the next 10 days." "Don't be ridiculous," she replied. In hindsight, she was probably in a bit of denial. But within just a few days, on 22 March, she heard that a friend had it, and by midnight the following Thursday, the 27th, South Africa was in lockdown.

Lockdown

Two days before lockdown hit, Dawn received a call from Mmusi Maimane from the OneSA Movement. He was looking for help delivering hand sanitiser and Covid-19 leaflets to educate communities on safety and preventative measures. Gradually, the enormity of the situation and the huge impact it would have on so many families who would be left without work, without food, and without the ability to socially distance, was coming home.

The next two weeks were a blur. To cope, we both started Deepak Chopra's 21-day Abundance Challenge – it made us feel centred and took our minds off the noise and uncertainty, but we also came to the realisation that the time had come to act. Dawn started making sandwiches and boiled eggs for a Cape Town-based soup kitchen, Ladles of Love, and Over the Rainbow decided to step in and help small businesses like ONEOFEACH sell their beautiful face masks.

Dawn spoke to entrepreneurs who were battling to survive, registered for every webinar she could find, and listened to podcasts that tackled a variety of Covid-19-related issues. And then she read a quote by June Crawford, a board member of the International Women's Forum South Africa, that redefined her thinking: "We can't predict our immediate future," said June, "but we can embrace the innovation of new ideas and the resilience that collective hope brings."

The Power of Hope

Dawn realised that she could be doing so much more to instil courage and positive reinforcement, a realisation that ultimately led her to starting online mentoring sessions to share innovative insights with entrepreneurs and to help them reengineer their business. It was then that Les called to suggest that that the Over the Rainbow team do more — that we write a book, a book on hope. It's this collection of hope stories that you are now holding in your hands.

While we continue to navigate our way through this crisis, we have come to the conclusion that, sometimes, hope is all we have. And yet, in its ability to inspire change and offer opportunity where once there was only uncertainty, there's no doubt of hope's immense and unfailing power.

Chapter 1

Passion

LIVE THE LIFE YOU WERE MEANT TO

Featuring:

- Dr Anwar Kharwa: Hospital of Hope
- Glynne Wolman: Angel Network
- Daniele Diliberto: Ladles of Love
- Karen Breytenbach: Soupa Group

"Hope is passion for what is possible."
—*Soren Kierkegaard*

"HUMBLE SERVANT OF THE PEOPLE"
by Dr Anwar Kharwa

About Dr Anwar Kharwa

Dr Kharwa, is a medical graduate who graduated from UCT in 1996. He then further specialised in family medicine and obtained this degree from the University of Stellenbosch in 2003. He then went on to obtain his MBA at the University of Stellenbosch in 2009. Currently, Dr Kharwa is the Senior Manager at the Department of Health, responsible for the development of Facilities Management – a broad based portfolio which impacts on all health facilities in the Western Cape. He was also responsible for the design, construction and commissioning of the Khayelitsha District Hospitals, the design and construction of Mitchell's Plain District Hospital, supporting the commissioning of Mitchell's Plain District Hospital and subsequent management of the Khayelitsha District Hospital.

The Approach

In early May 2020 I was approached by senior members of the Department of Health late on a Friday afternoon with the following request " Anwar, you are well aware of the Covid-19 pandemic, we need to set up a hospital at the CTICC in 4-weeks, that is your mandate, God help us all".

"Ok that's cool, I said – we'll do it!"

Not missing a beat they then asked "By when can we have the commissioning plan?" – note this was now after 4pm on a Friday afternoon. I then realised the urgency of this and committed to forwarding the plan to them no later than 4pm Sunday afternoon. This is the same plan we have worked on and that we have adhered to.

The Plan

We used department's standard Operations Management Accountability Framework which spells out the core principles for establishing a hospital. Although this is a field hospital for a specific purpose, it functions at a level of a big provincial hospital so that all administration, governance, clinical service protocols, quality protocols, supply chain and people management protocols are adhered to. We essentially implemented all these during the commissioning phase of this hospital.

4 weeks to complete

Construction began on the 11 May, our plan was as follows:

- Week 1 — This was all about the planning and design phase of the Hospital.

- Week 2 — Rapid construction and commissioning of all systems. This included Infrastructure, Information Technology, Information Systems, Health Technology, the Facilities Management aspects, People Management, Finance, Supply chain management — and so on. We pulled together a commissioning team of about 40 people who represented a broader stakeholder group from various departments from both all sectors of government. We convened on a weekly basis to deal with red-flags.

- Week 3 — Ward fit out, training, testing of systems.

- Week 4 — Go Live..! 8 June.

The rest is history — we opened the hospital 4-weeks later with our first patient on the 8 June. It went exactly as planned.

Hospital of Hope

Today, (18 June 2020), we have 65 patients on board. I think the Rainbow of Hope aspect and the collaboration with the schools for the 600+ Rainbow posters has been a beautiful, innocent collaboration with deep inspiring messages to patients and staff from innocent youngsters. To see our Premier Alan Winde, our President Cyril Ramaphosa, the Head of Department Dr Keith Cloete and senior members of government reflecting on some of these messages of Hope was truly inspiring. Although we are in this Covid-19 pandemic, the message to the patients is that you are in recovery and there is light at the end of the tunnel – and we at the Hospital of Hope are here to serve you.

When we started this project, the Team coined a vision statement: The CTICC and this Field hospital will be a symbol of Hope, Recovery, Strength, Humanity and Care. In a nutshell – this is the "Hospital of Hope".

Current Status

As with any new car, we are now monitoring and tweaking the systems as we go. You have a plan but when you implement the plan you may have to make a few changes based on operational requirements. It's also about fine tuning the systems to ensure you have a lovely "Purring Engine".

Within a week of opening, we have already admitted 65 patients. They are all in recovery and the feedback that we have received so far from patients is that the care is excellent. This is what we have planned for and aspired to when we commenced with the project. Although we have this dreaded virus and thousands of patients across the globe have passed away, once you enter this facility we want to make sure that you are going to walk out. That is the symbol of hope, humanity, empathy and the quality of care that we are aspiring to provide at the "Hospital of Hope".

The Hard Work has paid off

We had 14 sub-project teams behind the scene, each working around the clock, 24/7 – There was a lot of blood sweat and tears and personal sacrifices that have been made in order for us to ensure we delivered this "Hospital of Hope" on time and within budget.

Luckily we had the experience in the team to ensure a smooth operation.

One of the most significant moments for me was the official opening — blessed by the presence of the Premier, Senior members of the Western Cape government, National Government officials and our President Cyril Ramaphosa — To me that was the cherry on the cake.

Some Facts about the Hospital of Hope:

- It is fully digital.
- Originally planned for 850 beds but we have managed to squeeze in 862 beds.
- No visitors are allowed.
- More than 300 nurses are expected to work here.
- All systems are geared to reducing pressure on our land-fill and we have gone paperless.
- All systems are geared towards reducing the transfer of Covid-19.

Message of Hope

If we work together as a society and live up to our social values, our principles and with a focus on humanity and respect we can beat this. Even though we come from different cultures and different ethnic backgrounds what I have learnt in healthcare is this: When a patient is in an ICU bed, in that golden hour your ethnicity, your culture, your background does not play a significant role, it is then when our humanity, our care and our respect comes to the fore — to save human lives.

Covid-19 can be beaten. As long as we adhere to the basic guidelines and principles and we respect each other: The basic practices of hand washing, social distancing, wearing your face mask. These are the simple principles which we should aspire to on a daily basis. If we adopt this attitude we will overcome this virus and lives will be saved.

As the "Hospital of Hope" we are proud of the environment we have created. It's been a beautiful process and one of which myself and the team are truly proud of.

At the end of our interview Dr Kharwa showed me a short video clip of the first patient arriving just a few weeks ago. It was quite chilling to watch the convoy of emergency vehicles, the ambulance arriving, the line up of the medical professionals, all ready to serve and do their duty. I left feeling that HOPE is definitely ALIVE in this extraordinary "Hospital of Hope".

THE NINE MILLION RAND MIRACLE
by Glynne Wolman

About Glynne

After completing a Bachelors of Social Science Degree at the University of Cape Town, Glynne Wolman worked in both London and Israel, where she studied hotel management. On returning to South Africa in 1990, she began her career in recruitment in Johannesburg and, 10 years later, she and friend Leigh Brouze started their own agency. In 2006, they also launched a branch of the Jewish Women's Benevolent Society. In November 2015, Glynne founded The Angel Network NPO, and in 2017 she was nominated for the Absa Jewish Achievers: Jewish Woman in Leadership Award.

My Calling

I had always wanted to be involved in charity work, and was in awe of a woman named Rayna Levin, whose philanthropy I admired. She inspired me to be giving and hardworking.

The first project I initiated in November 2015 was a collection of toiletries for children in state hospitals. Within five days we had enough for 500 toiletry bags. I rallied my community mommies, who came to pack these bags and it was here that the idea of starting an NPO was sparked. In November 2015, we started The Angel Network.

In the early days, there were no money donations; we collected sports equipment, school shoes, Easter eggs, blankets and Christmas gifts from all kinds of sources to distribute to those in need. In the past four-and-a-half years, we have evolved so much that we've been able to assist people to start their own businesses, acquire hearing aids, prosthetics and glass eyes, and we even raised money for a child to have a kidney transplant. We didn't need to look for those who needed help – we put ourselves out on

Facebook and people found us. Initially we had 1 000 members, today we have approximately 25 000.

Today, The Angel Network is a registered non-profit organisation. Our goal is to facilitate acts of kindness and offer assistance to established welfare organisations. The focus is on giving a hand up, rather than a handout.

We receive no government funding, and do not incur any operating costs. Every cent donated is given directly to our beneficiaries. We are wives, mothers, aunts, nieces... We are everyday citizens who want to make a meaningful difference to our communities and our country. We have been going for over four years and my garage is our warehouse. We have branches in Johannesburg, Durban and Cape Town, and have been able to extend our reach to Mpumalanga, North West and Limpopo.

To date, we have helped to feed, clothe, transport, house and educate over 30 000 South Africans across six provinces, with over 50 beneficiary organisations in Gauteng.

The R9 Million Angels

Once Covid-19 hit us, I found myself working 14-hour shifts with about 15 WhatsApp messages an hour, 100 emails and 50 calls a day. In the first week of March, we spent about R350 000 on education, books, school uniforms, shoes, stationery and crafts. A small portion of the money went to sanitisers and emergency apparel, but at this early stage no one was asking for food donations. This all changed in April, when we were suddenly overwhelmed with requests for food. Because so many people weren't able to work during lockdown, they weren't earning any money. They might queue all day for a food parcel, only to be told once they get to the front of the line that the food is finished. Children who were starving were eating dog food, and fathers were contemplating taking their own lives as they couldn't even provide their children with a slice of bread.

Prior to the spread of Covid-19, the requests were more for education, clothing, sick children and so on – not for food on such a massive scale.

Miraculously, in April, we received two contributions from the South African Jewish Board of Deputies (SAJBD) to the value of R9 million. The SAJBD had originally received the donation and chose to partner with us to distribute it to the most marginalized in our country.

The majority of our money is currently being spent on food. We have come across a wonderful product called e'Pap, which contains all the nutrients required for an entire day in one bowl.

Life is unbearably hard for the majority of South Africans. Many of us don't realise how bad it is and what starvation really looks like.

Wisdom from the Frontlines

Some of the lessons and skills that I have learnt through this crisis include:

- Better time management. I am generally an organised person but this has become critical as there is so much on the go. I no longer waste time on long conversations. I get things done quickly and efficiently, and I always complete the most important tasks first.

- Not to take prejudice personally. I am exposed to it from all groups almost daily.

- Turn R10 into R100. I have learnt how to stretch a budget through the art of negotiation.

- To be flexible. We have had to redefine what our roles entail — we're no longer simply 'executive Angels', but also handle admin, funds, collections, distribution, food and requests.

- Remain human. One can almost become desensitised to the needs of others when it is all you are doing, all day every day.

For Everyone, by Everyone

Our community has always looked after one another and this has spilled over into The Angel Network, where our ethos can be summarised as "for everyone, by everyone". There is transparency, and our community trusts us.

One of my favourite quotes is from Helen Keller who said, "Alone we can do so little, together we can do so much." We are all in this together, we need to be there for one another, to take care of ourselves and each other. We all experience anxiety, fear, stress and hunger. We need to keep going and remain compassionate, kind, caring and considerate. Our chances of survival as a society are enhanced when we think beyond ourselves and help others.

The Starfish Parable

I love this story: one day, an old man was walking along a beach that was littered with thousands of starfish that had been washed ashore by the high tide. He came upon a young boy who was eagerly throwing the starfish back into the ocean, one by one. Puzzled, the man looked at the boy and asked what he was doing. Without looking up from his task, the boy simply replied, "I'm saving these starfish, Sir".

The old man chuckled aloud, "Son, there are thousands of starfish and only one of you. What difference can you make?" The boy picked up a starfish, gently tossed it into the water and, turning to the man, said, "I made a difference to that one!"

As Victor Frankel said, everything can be taken from us but the last of human freedoms: to choose one's attitude. Let's choose optimism, positivity, humility and hope. This is my calling. It's what I was meant to do.

Message of Hope

"Our chances of survival as a society are enhanced when we think beyond ourselves and help others."

Connect with us here https://theangelnetwork.co.za

SEVA
by Daniele Diliberto

About Daniele

> *Born in Zimbabwe, Danny Diliberto moved to South Africa as a teenager where he discovered his lifelong passion for food. It was after he left school to study a marketing course and earn some pocket money, working part-time, that he realised he wanted to work in the hospitality industry. Here he remained for many years until he finally decided to move on to Ladles of Love on a full-time basis at the end of July 2019.*

A Simple Gesture

Born into a Mediterranian family, food was a huge part of my early years – and so cooking, feeding and making people feel welcome all came naturally to me and led me into a career in food.

Ladles of Love began when I was inspired to create a project to give back to society, as a result of attending a course through the Art of Living Foundation (AOL) in Cape Town. As part of the course, attendees were encouraged to head out into the streets of Cape Town to offer hot tea to homeless people. As a restaurateur, I decided to make use of my kitchen and cooked up a fresh pot of soup. Walking the streets of Cape Town on a mission, I spotted a homeless individual walking along – the man was wrapped in a dirty duvet and was shouting and swearing as he went. I approached him to offer the soup, and in that instant, I saw how such a simple gesture had great power. The man stopped his shouting, accepted the soup, and thanked me before continuing on his way.

I realised that a moment of compassion and empathy had the power to restore dignity, even if just for a moment. I decided just to go for it, and at the first soup kitchen on a chilly July evening in 2014 a small team of volunteers served 70 hot meals in St Georges Mall outside my restaurant then, Doppio Zero. We set up a serving table on the boulevard, sent out some volunteers on bicycles to go look for those in need of a meal in the vicinity, and started serving as they queued in front of the table. Over the next five years, this grew to four soup kitchens, four schools and four other beneficiaries that we started to support with their feeding initiatives.

In July 2019, I walked away from the restaurant business and decided to go full time into Ladles of Love. During my time at the restaurant, I managed to operate Ladles from the kitchen, but when it closed we were blessed with a donation of a fully functional kitchen at The Hope Exchange on Roeland Street. We were immediately able to move our kitchen there and start operations from our own HQ.

Mission Impossible

At the beginning of March 2020, when Covid-19 hit our shores, social distancing meant that serving soup at our kitchens became a challenge. Once lockdown was imposed, I felt deeply compelled to get food out to as many people as possible, but I had no idea how I was going to get the money and we realised that this virus was either going to make or break us as an organisation. After consultation with the City of Cape Town we were able to get the necessary permit to continue our operations as an essential service provider to the vulnerable. Slowly, donations started trickling in and more people began to volunteer.

I wanted to source and supply the ingredients for a healthy, nutritious soup to various soup kitchens and shelters, and get food out to the masses. I began working with NPOs on the ground and spreading the word that I would provide the ingredients if they could collect them. They could then prepare the soup in their own kitchens.

We started by creating serving points that the homeless could get to and we connected with various shelters in and around Cape Town to serve the food. Prior to lockdown, we were supplying 15 000 meals a month. Currently, in one week, we sent out 265 000 meals and have had to significantly adapt and expand our organisation to assist more people in need.

Initially, I was dealing with 1.2 tonnes of food output a week; today we are dealing with 50 tonnes of food a week and have 100 beneficiaries and NPOs that we provide support too. These primary beneficiaries assist a further 200 plus beneficiaries so in total we are assisting over 300 beneficiaries.

I Believe in Miracles

Through our social media channels, Ladles of Love has created a global network of donors and we have built an incredible organisation. It has been miraculous, and I believe that as you need you will be provided for. People have come together; we have built a team and we all believe that no one deserves to go hungry — it is imperative to get food out there. When you are driven from a place connected to your heart and soul, you become connected to a higher force and you become the vehicle for that. You do what you can today, the best that you can today, and you do it now. Think less with your head and feel more with your heart.

We have expanded in such a short time and the kindness we have experienced in lockdown has been overwhelming. In the midst of so much uncertainty, the CTICC has given us an industrial kitchen and a hall to use until the end of June completely free of charge. People are entrusting us with their donations and all vegetables have been purchased by using the donations that we have received.

The Business of Giving

Ladles of Love has been all about the volunteers, but now we need a bigger and better system. We have had to create a core team who assist us on a full-time basis for a fixed term for a stipend. We require different departments for each need and have created hubs. I've had to learn a lot of new skills in order to manage this logistics, and there are three things I want to ensure in our business going forward:

- We become sustainable. Ladles of Love needs to make a 'profit' to keep going, but our primary purpose must come from the heart. One's purpose must be pure and passionate to be sustainable.

- We remain present. Our ethos is: do what you can today, yesterday is gone and tomorrow never arrives.

- We cultivate gratitude. The soul of the organisation needs to be pure, real and humble.

Finding Purpose

As far back as I can remember, I wanted to start an organisation that would encourage people to live fully. I grew up with a soft heart, wanting to help. As a young boy my mom would send me to school with a lunchbox the size of a backpack and I would share this with the kids from the boarding house. When I moved to South Africa in 1981, I was 11 years old and had to move into a boarding school myself. I was put onto a tight pocket money budget of R5 a week which I would spend at the café across the road and by Monday afternoon, the money was finished. My lack of discipline with my pocket money meant I would have to go through two break times without lunch and would have to wait till after school to eat lunch, which meant I would often go through the day hungry. Maybe it was this that unknowingly directed me to my purpose and drive to assist those in need of food. But it is not about "me", it's about "we". Commit a small act of kindness, every day, and the world will become a different place.

Message of Hope

"Service & selfless efforts for welfare of all. Dedication to others."

Connect with us here https://www.ladlesoflove.org.za

AND JUSTICE FOR ALL
by Karen Breytenbach

About Karen

> *Karen Breytenbach is a PR and NGO consultant, with a background in journalism and philanthropy. In her early career she was a chief justice writer for the Cape Times, and later moved into PR, which allowed her to build up connections with a large network of companies involved in impactful projects around Cape Town. In April 2020, she founded the Food Response Collective, a three-way collaboration between civil society, government and private sector partners, to fight the Covid-19-related hunger crisis in Cape Town.*

Mobilising the Community

I have one foot in PR and journalism and the other in charitable non-profit work, and it was this and the fact that I live in District 6, that led me to a deep collaboration with this incredible community.

Led by the District 6 Working Committee (D6WC), the community – which has an amazing grassroots structure – recently won a landmark court ruling that is ensuring their return to the slopes of Table Mountain in the next three to four years. It is not only a housing project, it is an ambitious and holistic socio-economic restoration project that requires a multi-faceted approach. All three tiers of government and several of their departments, as well as many civil society and other organisations, are involved. Together they will be bringing to life a vibrant, sustainably designed and beautiful new District 6. I am involved in that project, on the PR and strategic vision side of things.

With the arrival of Covid-19, wage worker communities couldn't work anymore and the situation became dire quite quickly for the thousands of District 6 community members, who today are dispersed all over the Cape Flats. People were running out of money and out of food.

True to form, the District 6 community mobilised and set up many, albeit under-resourced, grassroots soup kitchens. Through my networks I reached out to dozens of people, one of whom led me to Andre Viljoen from Woodstock Brewery – which, under the new regulations, could no longer brew beer, but did have 3 000 litre tanks in which they could cook a lot of soup at great speed.

Andre agreed to partner with us and a few other NGOs to supply large volumes of soup daily to vulnerable communities on the Cape Flats and in the townships. Some of the community food serving sites were run by D6WC, others by Cape Town CAN affiliates, others by other organisations. We also brought the City of Cape Town on board to provide vehicles and logistical support. Very soon the initiative was in full swing, powered by more than 200 volunteers chopping a few tons of vegetables daily. We were able to feed between 6 000 and 10 000 people every day during the course of Stage 4 and into Stage 3 of the lockdown.

Feeding the Hungry

The biggest lesson for me through all this has been that a small idea can grow exponentially – and this one is still growing. Initially the task of feeding the hungry people of Cape Town felt insurmountable, but an initiative like ours is an act of unbridled hope. It has picked up momentum and despite many unforeseen challenges, we've kept going for more than five weeks so far. We hope it is making a real difference. We'll never really know if our soup saved lives, but one thing is for sure – we must refuse to give in to the pessimistic notion of futility. If we all do something, if we keep beating back disaster one day at a time, maybe people will be okay.

Compassion Trumps Fear

Every day that I have woken up during this lockdown I have felt my heart swell and the fear dissipate little by little. I firmly believe that South Africans are resilient and compassionate despite our divided country. We have an innovation X factor because of the challenging environment we live in. We always find ways and means to make a plan and get things done.

Lessons Learnt

There is power in human connection. If you're an entrepreneur or concerned citizen with a great idea that could make a difference, but you don't know how to pull it off, think of the ways you can network and connect to others who can help you bring your idea to life. Build new partnerships with organisations that inspire you – you don't need lots of prior connections or money. You just need a good idea, and friends who have friends, and business connections that have business connections, Google, social media, and a bit of chutzpah.

Message of Hope

"An initiative like ours is an act of unbridled hope."

Connect with us here https://www.positivedialogue.co.za

Chapter 2

Credibility & Purpose

BUILD YOUR BRAND

Featuring:

- Grant Doubell: GroundUp

- Tamburai Chirume: OneofEach

- Wesley Fredericks: Red & Yellow

- Mpho Mohaswa: Precious & Pearl

"Credibility is the art of accepting responsibility."
—*Julian Hall*

FROM THE GROUND UP
by Grant Doubell

About Grant

> *Grant Doubell has an entrepreneurial background with experience in everything from construction to marketing. He has been managing director of The Ground Up Company since 2011, and 'lives for the challenge of new business start-ups'.*

Ground Control

Our construction services business is called The Ground Up Company. We are a turnkey construction company, which offers services from design right through to implementation. We design, build, project management, procure and then follow through to facilities management as well. The construction industry has been in a dire place, and so when lockdown was announced it was a disaster for us. During lockdown there was no billable trade happening. Our core team of managers worked harder than we have ever worked before and we have had the chance to launch some of our dreams and ideas.

Prioritising New Platforms

Our goal is to develop a construction academy – and the truth is that this is something I have been messing about with for the longest time and lockdown has exposed just how far we were away from getting it right. Out of the Ground will be run as an NPO and will assist our teams and staff members to upskill themselves. The reality is that some of our staff are on an entry level wage and I want to improve this situation. The idea is that they will do sub-contract work for The Ground Up Company and learn to build better and be given the opportunity to be upskilled, and earn more money. Our intention is that it will be run as a separate entity and any money that is made will not be incorporated into the bigger business, but rather stay in Out of the Ground for the team to learn and grow. We want to be able to give money back to the guys that did the work. We want to try and instill that hard work really does pay more.

Other ideas we have revisited are: Instead of running procurement as part of our business, we are now running it as a separate entity called Procurement Partner – a business we feel will change the way that people do Projects.

We have also introduced an app based maintenance solution called Ground Control, that runs our maintenance and warranty tracking. The app allows us to do critical maintenance and we are able to trade in any one of the five levels of lockdown.

We realize that working from home is the new normal and have put the idea of working remotely to our staff. We have also improved our systems and processes to facilitate this.

We are working hard at these ideas trying our absolute best to keep up with whatever the uncertain version of our future looks like.

Taking Time to Give

I wanted to donate to a worthy cause, so I started looking for a company collecting money for masks. When I realized that it wasn't quite that simple, I connected with a few colleagues from my EO network and one member donated a domain and a website. Within 2 days people were able to pledge to either donate money, masks and other PPE, or register to become a supplier. Our platform is called donate4corona.co.za.

I spent many hours working in this space, and have realized that not only was I being helpful to those in need, but I got to see life from someone else's perspective and I have gained an appreciation and gratitude for my own life.

Cultivating Grit

This challenging time has taught me that you have to do the things you sometimes don't enjoy doing, and for me that was managing the financial tasks of my businesses. Fortunately, I had built a lot of trust in our teams of people and there was very little kick back when we had to discuss salary and wage adjustments. I have had to cut every cost that I can, and I have done this by considering every spend three times. I have been committed to doing everything possible to save every job as I value our employees as people, and all that they have done for me over the years.

I have learned to respect money all over again. You realize how quickly things can change when you don't have another job coming in and you are grappling with the unknown. Saving, putting provisions in place and cash flow preparation has been a hard lesson for me to relearn, and the realities have been humbling.

Procrastination is my enemy. I had managed to find so many ways to keep myself busy, but now in lockdown there is no customer to sell to, or have a catch up coffee with. I have had to really keep myself accountable as a leader of a team and as a business owner.

Lockdown has been a place of positivity and gratitude. I have an awareness about what other people don't have in their lives, and about the people who work for me and what they live through on a daily basis. I have stopped to take a look at my industry, where you have a director's salary and then the people working on the ground doing the day to day. I am distressed by the fact that I hadn't seen that as clearly as I do now. I am grateful to have cultivated a better understanding of all of this. I only see us coming back stronger and am super optimistic about where the future will go.

Message of Hope

"I have found this time to be a place of positivity and gratitude. I am optimistic about the future."

Connect with us here http://groundupco.co.za

BETTER TOGETHER
by Tamburai Chirume

About Tamburai

> *Tamburai Chirume comes from a fashion retail and styling background. She studied consumer science in retail fashion management and has worked with major fashion magazines such as Elle Bulgaria. She then joined the banking world, which has helped her conceptualise their ONEOFEACH dream to become a business reality. Today, Tamburai is the co-owner of ONEOFEACH, a Cape Town-based luxury handbag company that she established together with her mother, fashion designer and visual artist Pauline Chirume. ONEOFEACH uses ethnic prints, leather and natural fibres to create handbags and accessories that are singular works of art — only one item is made in each style per size. Tamburai is passionate about making an impact as an agent of change in Africa.*

Get Back to Work

At first Covid-19 seemed like a faraway problem, but the closer it drew to home, the more we had to start asking ourselves, "Are people going to be buying handbags during this time of crisis?"

My tipping point came when I was on a Zoom call with a group of potential investors. I'm usually confident and articulate, but I suddenly broke down and started crying. I just couldn't justify offering a new investment opportunity when I didn't know what would happen down the line. I felt so vulnerable.

Two decisions quickly followed. The first thing I did was set up "Creative Conversations", an Instagram live event that enabled me to talk to my customers, suppliers and peers to see how we could support one another. The second was the decision to turn things around and do something to support my business and the women we employ. We had to get back to work.

From Handbags to Face Masks

Our business had been slowing down considerably and staying afloat was becoming a challenge. In response, we decided to start making fashionable face masks. I have always wanted to create change and provide jobs, to be able to share my knowledge and experience, and to lead with empathy and kindness. Unexpectedly, Covid-19 provided me with this opportunity.

The first two weeks of our pivot were incredibly stressful. We were used to dealing with international clients and selling across various platforms, including retail and wholesale. Now we were dealing with local clients who were watching their pennies closely. But our new offering has since rallied, and has expanded our business's customer base in the process. We have set up a Shopify site and our online sales are increasing. While promoting our face masks, we have even attracted handbag sales.

Meaningful Support

I put so much of our success down to my mother, who has helped to keep me grounded – always, but especially now. My mom is my rock and reminds me constantly that hard work, gratitude and a sense of community are all-important. I now feel hopeful for the post-Covid-19 world. I'm drawing on the wisdom of the older people around me, remaining calm and holding on tightly to hope. I have faced hardships in my life before. I know we will survive this crisis.

Message of Hope

"Hard work, gratitude and a sense of community are all-important."

Connect with us here https://oneofeach.co.za

KNOW YOUR PURPOSE
by Wesley Fredericks

About Wesley

> *Wesley is the Managing Director of Red & Yellow Creative School of Business. He took on the role in 2017 after 15 years working in Retail, E-commerce and E-learning. He is passionate about making a difference in South Africa through education and feels extremely proud to be a part of the team at Red & Yellow. When he is not working he enjoys cooking, playing his guitar and spending time with his wife and 3 children.*

Red & Yellow

In the early 90s, the founders of Red & Yellow were frustrated by the skills and abilities of graduates coming into their advertising agency. In an effort to improve this, the Red & Yellow School of Logic & Magic came into being in 1994.

In 2017, we repositioned ourselves as the Red & Yellow Creative School of Business. We are a creative thinking environment and I am extremely proud of the opportunities we offer to those who want to learn. We also pride ourselves on our 13-to-1 lecturer-to-student ratio, our online courses and qualifications, and the corporate training we provide.

A very Different Place

I will never forget 5 March. It was the day the first Covid-19 case was identified in South Africa. I had been watching the media, and particularly Italy, knowing that when Covid-19 hit here, we would be in for a tough time. I kept thinking to myself, "Once this breaks, our world is going to be a very different place."

I remember reading a Harvard Business Review article that spoke about the sense of grief the world was experiencing as a result of the pandemic: the loss of normality, the loss of proximity to others, and the obvious financial impact. Before too long, we were experiencing this ourselves.

I like to have things under control but, under these circumstances, that simply hasn't been possible, and there have been days when I have wondered how all of this will end.

Digital Transformation

The Covid-19 crisis has forced us to shift face-to-face teaching in our full-time school to remote teaching. We have tried as far as possible to ensure that no student has been left at a disadvantage. Bursary students who don't have the necessary infrastructure in place, such as computers and Internet access, have been loaned desktops and are using their travel stipends to purchase data.

Fortunately, online teaching infrastructure is already in place at Red & Yellow as we pioneered online learning in South Africa in 2007, so our task has largely been to stay relevant and to push innovation. But even so, many of our lecturers have had to adapt their content and skills to this new environment. Covid-19 has been a huge driver of digital transformation globally and this can only be a good thing going forward.

Purpose

One of my lessons in this tricky time has been the importance of purpose. At Red & Yellow, our purpose is to change the world though education. I try to promote this both as an individual and as a leader.

In the Covid-19 era, we have been forced to live out our purpose by being adaptable. We have had to absorb new information, understand its implications and make the necessary changes. The ability to make fast decisions and alter them when new information comes to light has been important.

Tough Decisions

As a private higher education institution, the economic impact of the pandemic has forced us to make sacrifices in some parts of our business to ensure that our students' education experience is not hindered in any way. Cutting costs is not an exercise I enjoy but being decisive and putting measures in place early has meant that we have set ourselves up to weather the storm.

Making these difficult decisions quickly ensures that we bring the most value to the most people and I have been blown away by my staff's understanding during this time.

I read a book a while ago called *Time to Think* by Nancy Kline, and although it may sound counter to what I have just said about making quick decisions, giving myself the time to ponder, apply my mind and find the answers, has been essential. I have blocked out every Thursday afternoon from 12 until 5 to ensure I have this time.

Moving Forward

One of our frustrations has been trying to get our website zero-rated. This would enable our students to access the website for free. We believe this should be universal, and are currently waiting for feedback from the Department of Higher Education and Training, which is negotiating with various service providers to pick up these costs.

My message of hope for other small businesses is to know your purpose. There will be days when everything seems difficult and uncertain, but having your purpose clearly defined will be a source of inspiration and motivation to keep showing up and putting one foot in front of the other.

Message of Hope

"Know your purpose."

Connect with us here https://www.redandyellow.co.za

PUTTING CUSTOMERS FIRST
by Mpho Mohaswa

About Mpho

Mpho is a qualified Chemical Engineer, with nine years' experience in the oil and gas industry. She held different functional positions before advancing to middle management as a business developer. She holds a National Diploma in Chemical Engineering from the Vaal University of Technology and a short course in Brand and Marketing Management from VEGA School. She founded Precious and Pearl Brands *in 2017 to mass produce and sell ginger-based concentrate and ready-to-drink products under the brand name Ghemere. The Ghemere company model has now expanded to retail, online and resellers, offering a wide customer base for growth and brand visibility.*

Facing Reality

To maintain the authenticity of traditional ginger beer, I founded Precious and Pearl Brands, a business that manufactures gemere under the brand name Ghemere (I added an "h" because another company had already registered the rights to the word "gemere").

Gemere is a traditional non-alcoholic ginger beer that has been enjoyed by South African families from different ethnic groups for decades. It's more than just a drink, it's an emotional connection, hence the slogan "going back to our roots". Our product is a fusion of the old great taste with a new twist, to give a new flavour experience. The long-term vision is to make Ghemere a household brand that can be enjoyed any time. In February, we got a hint here and there of the Covid-19 virus, but at this time it felt very far away. In March, though, after the 21-day lockdown was announced, like many South Africans I found myself going through online news updates every hour; it was time consuming and draining. I was anxious about what the future would look like.

Quieting the Noise

The first two weeks of the lockdown were hard for me. I began to contemplate starting a new business, but luckily, early in the process I realised I had to bring myself back. Find routine, stay focused, stay true to myself and the brand, and not lose sight of my true north. I told myself, "You don't need to shift your pot of gold, it's still right here." I knew we had enough savings in the business to survive three to four months without any income, so this was the least of our problems. We have always planned for rainy days, because today it might be Covid-19 but tomorrow it will be something else. It's important as a business to always have liquid cash savings. Another thing we did right as a company is to keep our monthly costs low and our team small; we are still in the growing phase.

The Marketing Pivot

The next important focus was to try to keep our old customers and attract new ones. As a customer-orientated business it was important — and still is important — to constantly communicate with our customers. Social media has been a great tool to connect. Now more than ever, the customer is king. We needed to increase customer service levels and add extra value.

What we did before the lockdown was to offer credit to our trusted resellers, and that paid off nicely. Resellers buy from us at a discount, and they sell for extra income. The challenge with this model is that for orders outside Gauteng, we used to deliver the product via taxis because this is a cheaper option for 20+ five-litre bottles, and so during this period it was difficult to deliver. We were forced to find alternatives, such as offering credit so that resellers have enough stock to last longer.

They say a crisis can be a jump forwards or a leap backwards, depending on your attitude. The new normal for us as a business was to adapt to change and review our online offering as well. This has helped us to tap into a new market we would not have considered accessing. We will soon be selling on Takealot! We have also used Facebook post boosts more now for brand visibility, and hopefully turn that into sales.

The media hype around staying healthy and hydrated in order to fend off Covid-19 played into our hands. We did a video explaining that you could add hot water to our Ghemere and add lemon and honey, and use this as an immune booster. As part of our marketing strategy we are looking at different ways our customers can drink Ghemere as an immune booster during the flu season.

We also understood that people were staying at home and baking, and scones go very well with Ghemere, so we introduced a smaller two-litre bottle so that we can cater for families (Ghemere is usually sold to cater for larger gatherings). We would not have thought of this without lockdown. So we are now concentrating on home consumption and trying to understand how to be top-of-mind on consumers' grocery lists.

In May, we approached the Food Lover's Market to stock our two- and five-litre bottles. Despite being in a crisis, we were offered an opportunity to do a tasting or promotion and people were open to trying it. Our product is now stocked in three of their stores. This means partnering with bigger retailers is an option going forward, but we'll still keep our resellers to balance our cash flow.

The alcohol ban has also worked in our favour and our customers have been creative with their Ghemere mix. Financially, we've managed to hit an upward trend and we hope this continues. We have started scheduling home deliveries into certain areas and are constantly looking at different ways to boost and promote our product.

Reaching Out

Being a mom to a four-year-old and a nine-year-old during this time has been challenging. My kids are used to playing outside and we have had to keep them indoors and entertained. We've had to have some form of structure and routine so that they would not lose momentum with their school work. I had to be available for my kids, to take on the role of being my four-year-old's teacher while still running the house and my business. I was finding it difficult to maintain a balance. My husband has had to step in and take care of my older child and we've been trying to get our rhythm back, getting closer to each other and helping each other by working together as a team.

My family has been a great source of strength for me, and so has the community of great entrepreneurs I surround myself with. Now, more than ever, we need a strong support system. Our mental health should be top priority.

Listening to different podcasts and live series hosted by different institutions has also helped me to stay focused. Everybody is learning how to live with this crisis and make a plan.

Life is Never a Straight Line

If we look hard enough we are sure to find hidden gems of opportunity. Never give up and don't be scared to ask for help — often, things are difficult before they get easy. The road to success is always under construction.

Message of Hope

"If we look hard enough we are sure to find hidden gems of opportunity."

Connect with us here **www.preciousandpearl.co.za**

Chapter 3

Action

BACK YOURSELF AND DO WHATEVER IT TAKES

Featuring:

- Vincent Viviers & Enrico Ferigolli: Bottles
- Jessica Boonstra: Yebo Fresh
- Roger & Matthew Fitzsimons: Happy Hygiene
- Dustin Botha: Luks Brands

"I find a reason to hope in any situation."
—*Anonymous*

MESSAGE IN A BOTTLE
by Vincent Viviers and Enrico Ferigolli

About Vincent and Enrico

Vincent Viviers graduated from the University of Cape Town with a Business Science Honours Degree in Marketing before honing his craft at some of the biggest and best companies in the world (Unilever, Google), where his passion for marketing in a digital age grew.

Enrico Ferigolli spent six years at Unilever in Italy and South Africa, then – answering a calling to learn more about the digital world – joined Gorilla Creative Media as Business Unit Director and Board member. Viviers and Ferigolli joined forces to become co-founders and co-CEOs of on-demand delivery app Bottles in 2016.

Find the Problem, Develop the Solution

It all started with a bunch of friends standing around the braai in 2015. Having run out of alcohol, the conversation went like this: "Imagine if we could press a button and drinks could magically appear?" In 2016, we forever altered South Africa's alcohol retail landscape by launching the first on-demand alcohol delivery app and service: Bottles.

Before Bottles was conceived, Vincent had combined his retail and tech experience from stints at Unilever and Google to forge his own entrepreneurial path with his digital tech startup, while Enrico converted the six 'extremely formative and fun' years at Unilever in Italy and South Africa, and the digital and business acumen he gained at Gorilla Creative Media, to build and scale his platform-based business. After meeting and becoming best friends during our time at Unilever, we joined forces to pitch our idea to business reality TV show *Shark Tank* in 2016, which enabled us to realise our Bottles ambitions and shake up a legacy industry where technology was virtually absent. This first investment of R1 million, coupled with our business mentors Gil Oved and Ran NeuNer, enabled us to embrace the entrepreneurial spirit. Our second investment, from the owners of the premium liquor retailer Norman Goodfellows, gave us an insight into the workings of the liquor industry. Then, in mid-2018, we partnered with Pick n Pay Liquor to scale the business and cement our place as the leading on-demand alcohol delivery service in the country, sourcing from over 60 Pick n Pay Liquor stores nationwide.

The Power of Partnership

The unprecedented pace and scale of Covid-19's economic impact has forced both small and large businesses to adapt or die during the lockdown. Of course, Bottles took a double hit when the government banned alcohol sales. Its survival hinged on quick, innovative thinking.

We took our four years of experience in building and scaling an e-commerce company, and expanded our existing partnership with Pick n Pay Liquor to create an on-demand, same-day Grocery Essentials delivery service in a matter of days.

Four days into lockdown, Bottles and Pick n Pay's online team leveraged the app's existing integration into the retailer's stock management, invoicing and reconciliation systems to pilot the grocery service. The proof of concept was small, using two stores to offer a limited basket of 150 items, but the response from registered Bottles users was overwhelming.

Business quickly boomed. We doubled our reach and trebled our volume of orders in a few weeks. Two months in, Bottles is consistently ranked within the top five apps in the Food and Drink category and within the top 20 apps overall in South Africa.

Tipping the Scales

This success prompted the team to rapidly upscale, expanding the new Grocery Essentials service across more than 90 Pick n Pay stores from Johannesburg to Pretoria, Durban, Cape Town, Bloemfontein and Port Elizabeth, with many other cities planned to launch soon. The range has also been extended to over 3 500 products, with more items being added every week based on customer demand. The service offers contactless same-day delivery, with an average delivery time of under 90 minutes.

As e-commerce continues to boom during the lockdown, our company is enjoying exponential growth. It has more than doubled its reach and has trebled its order volume in a matter of weeks, while giving customers an efficient and safe way to stay home and top up their grocery essentials. It is evident that more and more customers are wanting to shop from home, and we've scaled the service effectively to cater to customers' needs.

Key Learnings

Through this experience of growth and change, we discovered the crucial importance of:

- Resilience. It doesn't matter how hard your day was, when you wake up the next day you have to do it all again.

- Partnership. Having a partner is a huge asset. There are a lot of dark moments and challenges, and having someone to share the journey with who has worked alongside you is priceless.

- Perseverance. We thought it was all over, until we found a way forward. Now, more than ever, we have to persevere and negotiate the roadblocks.

- Team and culture. We could not have pivoted so successfully without our staff. They have pulled together and made it happen in record time. Our team felt like they were part of the solution.

Big Change = Big Opportunities

Entrepreneurs need a high appetite for risk. We understand that lots of people will lose their jobs, and we have to step up and grow the economy and solve problems. We need to find solutions to the myriad issues that are going to rise out of this crisis. This is a time of big changes in society. We are not like our corporate friends, who close their laptops at 5pm. We have to take this opportunity to make something different. We can't allow our fears to hold us back; this is our time.

Message of Hope

"We can't allow our fears to hold us back – this is our time."

Connect with us here https://bottlesapp.co.za

THE UNLIKELY ENTREPRENEUR
by Jessica Boonstra

About Jessica

> *Jessica Boonstra is the founder and CEO of Yebo Fresh, an online shopping service that delivers popular groceries to townships and other areas that are generally unserved by most formal retailers. Born and raised in Holland, Jessica completed an MSc in Engineering and embarked on a career in logistics at Shell, followed by several roles as senior manager and director at Ahold. She moved to South Africa in 2015 and cofounded South African/Dutch consulting company Alchemize in 2016, as well as Buzzer Community Safety, an emergency services app. In 2018, her pride and passion, Yebo Fresh, was born and continues to grow from strength to strength.*

A Fresh Start

When I met my husband at my first job at Shell, we discovered we shared a love of travel, and as a young married couple, we wondered, "Why are we working so hard to travel?"

Five years ago, as a family, we (my husband and our three kids, then 9, 7, and 5 years old) decided to sell our home, our BMW, let go of our comfortable lifestyle and embark on an adventure: we moved to Cape Town.

Our friends thought we were crazy. Both of us thought we would find jobs easily, but we didn't. It was a tough time as both of us struggled to find employment, and being foreigners we didn't have a network. We resorted to doing all kinds of jobs — at one stage we were having to sell our kids' toys in order to make enough money to buy groceries, it was a crazy time. We so loved this place, we were determined to stay.

During this time, I volunteered in some of the townships and I also did consulting work for some retailers. I started connecting the dots, because there was a huge gap around access to food delivery and groceries in the townships. There are not enough opportunities to buy quality food and many of the retailers are focused on the high-end market. I was talking to some of the large chain store brands and one of their proposed strategies to attacking the middle and lower market was building more stores, but this is impossible as the townships are already overcrowded.

Find a Way

I found an investor, a connection I'd made through volunteer work and he said: "If you have an idea, I'll fund you." I replied: "But I'm a corporate girl and have no idea how to run a business!" He just told me to give it a try, go ahead and do it. This was 18 months ago, in 2018, and so that's how Yebo Fresh began.

It's an online shopping service; we deliver popular groceries straight into areas that are generally unserved by most formal retailers. This has been quite a journey. We started by talking, listening and tuning in to the residents of Imizamo Yethu to discover what they wanted with regards to groceries. We got a better understanding of their tastes and preferences and began experimenting.

We started off using my garage in Hout Bay and turned this into a storage unit for the groceries before delivering them to the various households.

We connected with more and more investors who believed in the concept and by February 2020, we had a good base system up and running, and had started expanding into Khayelitsha, Langa, Guguletu and Delft.

The power of what we do lies in that 90% of our staff are from the townships. People phone or go to the website and place an order, the orders are packed and the drivers – also from the townships – deliver the goods. The uniqueness of our company is that we understand the township shopper; we treat our customers like VIPs and we give them the full service that they deserve. We have employed 40 people as well as drivers who all own their own bakkies. A monthly shop can be upwards of 60kg and more often than not, a full load of eight tons is sent out for delivery. We deliver both large and small volumes. Initially we were delivering to private customers, but lately we have started working with charities.

Answering the Call to Expand

When Covid-19 arrived, we got tremendous traction virtually overnight and we were not prepared for it at all. The phones did not stop ringing. Charities and individuals wanted to send food into the townships and there was no other service that allowed this on a large scale. Even for those who had money to buy food, queues outside the township supermarkets were so long it could take up to five hours to get inside. You can't practise social distancing like that, it's a disaster.

In February, we were processing 200 orders a month, and currently we are dealing with between 800 and 1 000 orders a day. Our business model and partnerships with manufacturers have allowed us to deliver top quality products and A-brands at extremely competitive prices. We are serving Imizamo Yethu, Langa, Khayelitsha, Mfuleni and Gugulethu. Following recent seed funding, we will soon be expanding across the greater Cape Town area.

A year ago we moved into a warehouse, which seemed so big at 180 square meters, yet this was slowly filled and within 10 days of lockdown we had to take over the neighbour's warehouse of an additional 400 square meters. Another 10 days later, we had to move into a warehouse of 1 200 square meters in Airport Industria, and again we have had to move into the building next door. Today we have one warehouse of 2 400 square meters – all of this in just two months.

Fortune Favours the Brave

It is really exciting and tricky being an entrepreneur. Every day we send out the equivalent of 100 000 meals. The responsibility of having so many people working for you, and having them go into areas that are densely populated is scary. I have been able to hire some amazing people, many of whom didn't have jobs. I have a new management team and I have had to learn to let go and trust them because it has become too big for me to manage alone. It has been amazing to sit back and see it all unfolding, and allowing others to step up and run with their own ideas. Our drivers have been attacked by hungry and angry people and the huge responsibility of keeping everyone safe and compliant is a challenge. On top of this, our customers are vulnerable – often older, sick, sometimes with unstable family circumstances – and our staff are exposed to this high risk every day. We have had to put certain measures in place, but things have happened so fast that we haven't had time to really think too much about the dangers. Growth keeps coming – we have guardian angels all over the place.

Fake it till you Become it

I became an entrepreneur by accident. I was forced to face all the things I was afraid of, like standing in front of a group of people and giving direction. Making tough decisions. These moments have caused me to grow the most – and they've been the most thrilling! For me, it's about humbly accepting this position and taking on the task that I have been given, facing my fears and just going for it.

I have had to learn to run this business. I was already used to running a budget, but now I am having to talk about valuation, funding, marketing, sales and PR, and manage our investors, all of whom are entrepreneurs themselves. This has really helped, as they are involved in the business and bring their skills to the table. They are good sparing partners and I feel well supported and fortunate.

I get really angry at people who paint township life as a picture of doom. My experience of people in the townships is that they are struggling, but they are positive and creative and are looking for ways to make it work. They have a rich food culture, music culture and art culture. Townships are dynamic and interesting and for me this is the future of the country. I would like so many more people to start innovating, there are so many entrepreneurs in the townships that deserve support and investment, and many more of us need to be looking into it. People need to change their perception.

Message of Hope

"Change your perception, the opportunities are there."

Connect with us here https://www.yebofresh.co.za

START MARCHING
by Roger and Matthew Fitzsimons

About Roger and Matthew

> *Twins Roger and Matthew Fitzsimons left school and went their separate ways, travelling the world and gaining experience. Today as business partners and entrepreneurs they are known to say, "We came from the same womb and are now working in the same room." Their businesses, Big Eye Branding (founded in 2006) and Promobasket (founded in 2017) were selling, manufacturing and supplying promotional items to companies and individuals in over 40 countries in Africa through Big Eye Branding.*

From Chaos to Clarity

When Covid-19 hit us, everything came crashing down. Our company, Big Eye Branding, went from functioning at full-throttle to 5% turnover in just two weeks. As you can imagine, our initial reaction was pure panic. But as we calmed down, we realised that even though our current business-as-usual was out the window, we still wanted to hold on to our core values: always blow customers away; get your heart pumping; dig deep and be real; put in more than you give; aim high.

Over the years, we'd built up a strong culture in our business and looked after our staff. Now that the crisis had hit us, we needed to lead with confidence and start marching towards a new future.

The Three-Step Action Plan

Right off the bat, we decided we had to do three things:

- Set a date. It didn't matter when the date was, it was more important to just pick a date — our thinking was that it would be easier to negotiate over a fixed timeframe. We chose a three-month period and made plans to have a big party on 16 June to give our staff something positive to look forward to. We negotiated wages (cutting or reversing increases) and rent.

- Reduce costs. We needed to cut our salary bill by 20% and reversed any recent increases. Not one person in our whole team resisted this decision and we realised we had the right team on board. We also introduced a four-day week so that people didn't feel short-changed.

- Send staff home. We challenged our staff to work from home, develop and grow. This took a lot of trust in our people to get on with their jobs, and they needed to trust us in turn to lead them into this uncertain time.

Gathering Intel

One of the first, most important things we did was make a list of all the brightest business minds we had access to, and began to pick their brains. We asked them: "Should we feel guilty about setting up a business in this space?" They told us that if we did not operate in this space our business wouldn't exist, and secondly, that we had a responsibility to operate in order to keep the market honest, to ensure that there is supply and to continue to contribute to CSI. Plus, we'd be fighting to keep our staff employed. One conversation that really stuck with me was with a friend from Australia who said, "By not getting involved, you are doing a disservice to your country."

We realised that we were a branding company, and that meant we are a communications company – in the past we were communicating about products like beer, coke, cigarettes and healthcare. Now we were communicating about a virus. We had to think carefully about where people were spending money and put our thinking caps on. We began to look around at what was happening in the rest of the world and to ask ourselves: "What will our world be like after Covid-19 has hit us?" We studied what companies were doing when they returned to work, who were ahead of us on the curve.

A New Business is Born

This is the time to thrive as an entrepreneur. We realised that once businesses were able to get back to work, there would be a real need for them to be compliant and keep their customers and staff safe. We asked ourselves: Why not build a marketplace and supply everything businesses will need?

In just four days, we conceived, built and launched a new company – without even sitting in the same room together! That company is Happy Hygiene, an e-commerce site that sells hygienic kits for businesses to use on their return to work. The kits ensure that each business is fully compliant and staff are kept healthy and safe. In 15 minutes, a manager can have a completely compliant business environment for his staff.

How did we do it? As a result of our inquiries, we were introduced to a supplier in China and began to import masks, thermometers and virus fighting equipment, and stored this in our warehouses. We then started working really quickly with our suppliers. On the Sunday we decided to build an e-commerce site and our young tech team were brilliant. By Thursday morning our first credit card transaction went through and in the first week we had 230 orders.

By mid-May, we had 2 500 people visiting our site every day. We have had a real window into the world of e-commerce and have been on a steep learning curve. We saw a need and have built something compelling – I think one of the secrets to our success is that we created this business like a campaign. It doesn't have to live forever, but we hope it will be around for a while.

We have white labelled our Healthy Hygiene brand and launched our site in Kenya. The real strength is on the marketing side, the ability to scale and get it seen. The plan is to roll this out into Africa. We usually have a few big orders and this new business is a whole different game: small orders, packaging boxes and getting things out fast. We are learning as we go. Everything is automated, we have embraced e-commerce and everything has changed so much, so quickly.

Not Just Another Product

One of our managers said that working on this new business makes him feel like he is doing something good, and that we are not just selling a product to make a quick buck. By helping businesses get back on their feet, we are helping the economy – and that feels so right. We have also linked up with the Robin Hood Foundation and there is an option that for every kit that is bought, a food parcel goes out to a less fortunate family on your behalf. For us, looking after communities is important.

As entrepreneurs we see opportunities coming out of these tough times and believe that business should be fun and exciting. It's important to be conscious of what media you consume and to start the day in a positive frame of mind. This could mean journaling, meditating or even just lying in your bed smiling before you start your day.

Message of Hope

"People are open to new ideas, and the time is now."

Connect with us here https://www.happyhygiene.co.za

THE HUSTLE IS REAL
by Dustin Botha

About Dustin

Dustin Botha is cofounder of Luksgroup with business partner Daniel Hoffman, and is the director of Luks — exclusive distributors in Africa for Skullcandy, LAMY, Ogio, Traeger Grills, Velcro, Montegrappa and U-BOAT watches — and Luks Brand, which provides screen printing, embroidery and digital printing services, and also holds licences for the Springboks, Uflex headwear, Dustees premium garments and Smiley World.

Working the Network

I started my working career in a warehouse (Pulling & Packing orders and dispatching Stock) directly after school. My break came when one of the sales reps suddenly resigned from the company. I was asked to fill in and merchandise her stores. After a week of pounding pavements the owner of the business handed me my petrol card and two order books. He said don't came back to the office until the order books are full. I ended up in Botswana a week later asking them to send me more order books. After about a year of learning every aspect of the business I went on to work for Billabong. I started my agency with 1 brand and a 30 sqm office. Fast forward 7 years we were one of the biggest brands in the country and we had a stable of 7 brands (Billabong , Element , Vonzipper , Nixon , Kustom , Palmers and DC shoes) Myself and my business partner Daniel Hoffmann had been working by day and building Luksbrands by night. We would meet for dinner check the orders that had come in and then go off and prepare / pack orders all night long. We had stock to the ceiling in every spare space we could find, including my bathtub. It was a trip ...

Being the hustler and a serial entrepreneur, my partners recognised my skill and understood that the apparel bug has never let go of me and gave me the freedom to focus on a new mask making business. One of my business involvements was with a screen printing and embroidery company, an industry in which a lot of my past experience lies. When lockdown hit, I decided to go down the rabbit hole of sourcing fabric, embroidery and elastics for this business, using the contacts that I'd built up over the years. Due to the Level 5 and 4 restrictions, secret meetings in underground parking lots were set up in order to get what we needed from the fabric fairies.

Some of our staff from Luksgroup put their hands up to assist with this project – which now falls under a new branch called "Luks Brand" – and the wheels were set in motion. New friendships have been forged, new relationships are being built and new businesses are emerging as we set up the supply chain. We literally built the parachute as we were falling!

The Perfect Pivot

Despite the fact that this has all been done under cover, our local production is in full swing and our industry is alive and kicking. We are delivering a ton of masks into the market and have acquired all the necessary certification. We don't need to import goods. Trading directly to the customer and taking out all the fat in-between is where it's at.

It feels like I have gone back to my roots as 'Dustin the trader', making literally hundreds of calls every day. I know that I can't wait for things to come to me, I am putting myself out there and I know help is available from the connections and relationships I've taken care to cultivate over the years.

The Key is Trust

I have three kids and a fiancé, and I have got to support my family. No matter how bad it is, the sun will come up every single day. My daily challenge is to focus on staying calm and trying not to overcomplicate things. For me, the no.1 key is trust. In times like this trust becomes your business currency.

My "love language", if you like, as an entrepreneur, is relationships – if you look after your relationships on a daily basis, when a crisis hits you'll have a network that is built on trust that you can call on. Now more than ever, it's so important to maintain and nurture your business relations with intentional communication. People don't support businesses and products – people support people.

Message of Hope

"My advice to other entrepreneurs who may be struggling at this time is to pick up the phone and call as many people as you can, people you trust or look up to, and speak to them. You don't have to know them personally. You can even call me! For advice, insight, ideas and encouragement. Don't be scared to look people up and approach them with questions or ideas. Every great business idea, for me, has come through a conversation. Build the parachute!"

Connect with Dustin here https://www.linkedin.com/in/dustinbotha/

Chapter 4

Love What You Do

INNOVATE AND PROSPER

Featuring:

- Vusani Ravele: Native Decor

- Dr Jedd Meyers, Rafeea Peer & Ntombizodwa Nyoni: HealthInsite

- Alon Sachs: Mobelli

- Takura Chimbuya & Vizolet Kuwanda: Brothers Beard

"Hope is the beacon which points to prosperity."
—*Edward Councel*

DIY TO AR
by Vusani Ravele

About Vusi

> *Native Décor is the brainchild of Vusani Ravele, who started the business as a part-time hobby from his living room in 2015 after receiving a cordless drill from his girlfriend for Valentine's Day. Vusi soon found that he simply couldn't stop making and drilling holes into things. Fast-forward a year and he was making history on M-Net's Shark Tank SA TV show. He became the first entrepreneur to benefit from a lucrative investment deal with his present day business partner, Gil Oved of the Creative Counsel. Today, Native Décor creates visually appealing products that are both innovative and functional using sustainable timber. Its style is minimalist and inspired by our beautiful country, South Africa.*

Seeing the Wood for the Trees

Native Décor started small, but within a few months we'd started to land great deals with the likes of Yuppie Chef, eBucks and Zando. Two years later, our products were available on Takealot and Superbalist as well. Initially, we were producing small pieces of furniture such as bedside tables, but by the end of 2019 we were starting to make a bigger impact and larger items were added to our product line.

In January 2020, the threat of Covid-19 seemed far away. But by March, the realisation of how serious it was started to hit, as well as how severely it was likely to affect businesses. When we went into lockdown towards the end of March, no one knew what was going to happen. Everyone started panicking. I had just ordered a load of stock and all of our orders were suddenly cancelled.

In March, we lost 30% of our business and a further 50% in April. I emptied out our bank account to pay my staff. Now I had to figure out a way to pivot our business mid-lockdown as I had just hired an industrial designer and needed to justify the extra cost. We communicated daily to discuss how we were going to redesign our range.

The Pivot

In those first five weeks of lockdown, I had a warehouse full of stock, but no permit to go to work. I remember sitting at my desk watching our CCTV cameras and the delivery trucks driving past. We realised that people were stuck at home and were taking more of an interest in their environment — both their office space and their living space — and that we could *capitalise* on this opportunity.

We quickly got to work digitally designing our range of office furniture while remaining true to our African style. We put everything we created online. Our idea was to make new furniture that was light, easy to pack and assemble, and affordable — almost along the lines of an African IKEA.

We also started using augmented and virtual reality so that people could select one of our items and project it into their homes. This technology really is incredible: it enables us to bring our products to our clients, and allows them to view and even walk around their chosen item before buying it. During the most stringent periods of lockdown, we focussed our efforts on marketing our office furniture through our website, but now that e-commerce is available, we are able to sell and deliver our entire range of products. To date, we have designed approximately 120 new products.

Seven Lessons Learnt

The lessons that I have learnt through this crisis:

- Manage your expectations and talk to people more experienced than you
- Expect to fail in your first business and know that there will be other opportunities down the line
- Innovate as often as possible
- Don't get comfortable or complacent

- Stay relevant
- Move fast if you're going to keep up with the digital age
- Believe in yourself

I have also learnt several new skills that have proven invaluable during this time. Learning to leverage the power of social media, for example, has been critical. In the past I would have gone to an agency, but circumstance meant that I had to manage our platforms myself. Now I go online every morning, design something interesting and post it. I have realised how powerful this medium is, especially if you stay authentic. I've loved the positive reactions we've received and feel like I have a lot more control over my business.

I've also shared some photographs of products we've delivered to clients as Instagram stories. Seeing what they look like in people's homes – and receiving great feedback online – has been an interesting and encouraging experience.

Ultimately, I've learnt not to get caught up in the negativity. Once lockdown eases, it will be a new world. Now is the time to start learning and building ourselves up to do the things we want to do after the lockdown period passes.

Words of Wisdom

At this point in history, we need entrepreneurs who are well informed, can validate their ideas, and are prepared to learn from others who have endured difficult times before. If you're an entrepreneur, ask for help, and validate, validate, validate. Remember that there is no need to reinvent the wheel. Be creative. We need African solutions to African problems.

Message of Hope

"Don't let lockdown get you down."

Connect with us here https://nativedecor.co.za

ON THE FRONTLINE
by Dr Jedd Myers, Rafeea Peer and Zodwa Nyoni

About Dr Jedd Myers

Dr Jedd Myers is the Chief Operating Officer at HealthInsite, one of the country's leading corporate wellness and occupational health service providers. HealthInsite's employee well-being programme delivers impactful solutions for organisations through its strong digital presence, its highly interactive online portal, and its personalised offerings. With a history dating back 20 years, HealthInsite has provided health interventions to over a million people in South African corporate, parastatal and governmental environments.

A Dual-Pronged Approach

HealthInsite has always embraced change and is constantly innovating to ensure that our clients receive industry-leading services and products. As a result, when Covid-19 struck, we realised that our expertise, capacity and resources were about to be more necessary and meaningful than ever before. We pivoted quickly, adjusting our wellness knowledge and programmes so that they could positively impact a much wider audience: the South African public at large.

We quickly set up two key interventions: the first was a Covid-19 hotline and the second a drive-through testing service. Both were aimed at addressing the swift rise in the number of cases in the country and to help alleviate some of the strain that laboratories were already starting to take.

Our Covid-19 hotline allows people to be screened and diagnosed telephonically, which helps to ensure that only those with Covid-19 symptoms are sent to be tested. It also incorporates a tracing service so that the people with whom positive patients have been in contact can be identified, screened for symptoms and encouraged to get tested.

Rafeea and Zodwa

Rafeea Peer, a qualified pharmacist, and Zodwa Nyoni, a registered nurse, are part of our Covid-19 response team, and both were on site the morning of our first drive-through test.

"I feel like I've had to adapt to this experience almost overnight," Rafeea says. "I'm online and on call 24/7 to ensure we deliver a seamless service. I'm also actively involved with how our business is going to have to evolve in order to continue to have a positive impact. We have to constantly keep up with the times if we're going to stay relevant."

At the same time, this experience has also been an incredible learning curve for her and has reaffirmed her passion for making a difference in people's lives, she says.

Zodwa admits that finding a balance between her work and personal lives was initially very difficult but with the support of the HealthInsite management style we were able to find our balance. "I'm part of the hotline team and navigating the early days of the pandemic, when everyone was very panicked, was stressful," she explains. "But things have become easier as time has passed, and my improved people management skills have stood me in good stead."

Helping everyone get through this time without being afraid has taken careful and dedicated attention, Zodwa adds, but having access to the latest information has helped immeasurably. "We're constantly researching changes in the pandemic's protocols to make sure that the information we pass onto our team members and clients is accurate and up to date," she says.

Drive-Through Testing

Our drive-through testing facilities allow people to be tested for Covid-19 from the comfort of their cars, preventing them from having any contact with other potentially positive patients. The system is also set up to ensure that they receive accurate test results in the shortest possible time frame.

The first drive-through testing site we set up at The Wanderers in Johannesburg took off immediately. About 30 cars arrived on day one, and the site now averages between 30 and 40 cars a day. On peak days, over 90 people are tested. A similar site has since been set up at The River Club in Cape Town, where an average of approximately 20 people are tested daily. Anyone who receives a positive result is contacted and referred to the national tracing process, which is monitored by the National Institute for Communicable Diseases (NICD).

During this process, we follow the strictest quality assurance guidelines and align with local and international best practice to keep our staff and patients safe. We also ensure that we work according to the prescribed NICD and National Department of Health guidelines.

We've also set up a mobile testing units that are able to test people who can't drive to a lab or to one of our drive-through testing stations. This includes people who are sick or for whom privacy is paramount.

Staying Relevant Amid Change

We know that we're going to have to keep a close finger on the pulse if we're going to continue to offer what people, health facilities and our government need, and we're really excited about the opportunity this offers us to be creative and innovative.

We also understand that in order to maintain this relevance, our people need to be our first priority. They are at the heart of our business – as they are in any business – and investing in their knowledge, skills and health will help to ensure our growth going forward.

Message of Hope

"If Covid-19 has taught us anything, it is that pivoting is critical in ensuring businesses' relevance and resilience, having a stable and well performing business allowed us to pivot quickly to capture the opportunities. As the economy starts to open up, new businesses will spring up and new industries will form, and those who capitalise on these opportunities will be the ones to

thrive. Assess your services, products and business model, make the necessary changes, and look beyond the obvious and ordinary. Even amid the chaos, there is success to be had through positive impact."

Connect with us here www.healthinsite.net

FIND A BETTER WAY
by Alon Sachs

About Alon

> *Alon Founded Mobelli Furniture and Living to solve a problem, which later evolved into a company that creates beautiful places and connects people. He is a strong believer that furniture is where friends and family gather; it is where stories are shared and where memories are made. All furniture that gets added to the collection must be hassle free, offer great comfort & ergonomics, be of value and be beautiful too. If it's beautiful but not comfortable you will not find it at Mobelli.*
>
> *As a result of his passion for customer delight, those who buy from Mobelli keep coming back for more. Mobelli imports its products from around the world, and is also proud to support locally produced merchandise. Many of its products are bought and made in South Africa.*

There is a Solution for Every Problem

I started Mobelli Furniture when I built my house. I was struggling to get great furniture at a good price and, when I did find something I liked, I often had to wait for ages for the supplier to get it in stock. I remember ordering a sun lounger, which the salesman told me I had to oil regularly. I duly did, even though it was hard work, but three months later it was winter and raining, and my sun lounger was basically falling apart.

I thought: there's a business here. I could do this better. I could make good-quality furniture that lasts and is affordable. And that's how Mobelli was born. We have been in business since 2006 and have built a great brand – our slogan is, "Inspiring Spaces. Creating Moments". People tell me that my business model is lousy because our furniture lasts too long!

Augmented Reality to the Rescue

We walked into 2020 with an aggressive expansion plan. We had just opened up a massive showroom in Fourways Mall in Johannesburg, and had hired an agency to do a national brand campaign for us. We wanted everyone in the country to know who we were. But when Covid-19 hit, everything shut down and we had to start thinking about how to keep our business afloat when we weren't allowed to deliver furniture.

We'd started exploring 3D visualisations a few years earlier, as well as live shows, which make use of augmented reality to digitise certain times. I hadn't heard of live shows at the time, and didn't know of anyone using them in South Africa. I started looking into the technology, and was impressed by how it allows people to see the furniture in our showroom projected into their homes. The experience is simple and seamless; there's no app required. Users simply select an item and, once it has been converted into 3D, they can interact with it virtually.

Our first live show involved our lotus grill, which customers could place digitally in their lounges and on their patios, while also receiving all the relevant product information.

The Future of Retail

We reopened our showrooms under lockdown level 4, which permitted the sale of home office equipment. Although many people were working from home at the time and were likely in the market for reliable office furniture, we realised that furniture purchases were still a luxury. We needed to get people excited about buying furniture again, which is why we put new energy into our augmented reality technology.

This technology has been accelerated by Covid-19. It has been the engine for change in our business. At the beginning of the year we considered doing tours around the country in a pantechnicon truck with a mobile showroom inside. Now that we could no longer bring people to our showroom – either stationery or mobile – at least we could take our showroom to the people. I believe this is the future of retail.

The Power of Collaboration

My brother and I work together. He is the realist, the one who makes things happen, and I am the visionary. He works on ensuring that we survive today, while I think about re-inventing the business for tomorrow. I think our integrated, complimentary partnership is going to be phenomenal for Mobelli.

We're creating a whole new business by leveraging off our old one. We're currently digitising our chairs and lounge furniture so that our clients can see these products too. We are the first in our industry to use augmented reality without the need for a specific app, and even though we've noticed a bit of hesitation in people adopting it, we're forging ahead.

Learning New Skills

I have learnt a lot about myself during this time. I feel like I'm building something innovative that I can hand over to my team to manage going forward. When you're hit with a crisis like this, you have to find a way to get around the brick wall. I never give up. I'm determined and I thrive on challenges. The regular day-to-day running of a business doesn't excite me.

I have had to learn a new skill in order to maximise my business's success: influencing people to come round to a new way of thinking, to use technology to acquire the products they need. I'm working on it every day.

I believe the future looks good for us. People are more likely to stay home and have "staycations" and will take more interest in their environments. People will buy better quality products and they will buy fewer products — and that's exactly the space in which we play.

Our Realisation

This is what I've come to realise during this crisis: if you're faced with a problem, spend time thinking about it, verbalise it, talk about it, and write it down on a piece of paper. If you do, the solution will come to you.

We've built a great brand and have managed to create a personalised experience for our customers. Going forward, our aim is to catapult people into a new way of thinking.

Message of Hope

"Catapult yourself into a new way thinking."

Connect with us here https://mobelli.co.za

LOOK GOOD, FEEL GOOD
by Takura Chimbuya and Vizolet Kuwanda

About Takura and Vizolet

Takura has spent the majority of his professional career to date in Standard Bank's corporate investment banking division, optimising and streamlining the bank's financial reporting, insights and functional analytics processes. He is passionate and motivated by the promise that technology, data and innovation holds in helping millions of Africans leverage their entrepreneurial energy, and how technology will affect and effect change on the African continent. In his spare time, he works on his passion projects, graphic design and photography, and continues to support the European Champions, Liverpool. Takura is a mechanical engineer and an alumnus of the University of Cape Town.

Vizolet started off his career in auditing and accounting at Deloitte in Johannesburg where he gained experience in a number of different industries, primarily aviation and aerospace. He has since joined the College of Accounting at Monash University as an adjunct lecturer. Vizolet is passionate and motivated by the power of cross-cultural collaboration among youth as a means of solving some of the most pressing economic and social issues that we face in Africa. In his downtime, he enjoys cooking and watching Arsenal mess with his feelings. He holds a chartered accounting degree from the University of Cape Town.

A Gap in the Market

We've been helping men to care for and groom their beards under the Brothers Beard brand since 2016. Our idea was born when Takura — better known as TK — realised that he could never grow a proper beard because he always shaved it off just as it became itchy and scratchy. With his engineering background in hand, he did some market research and joined forces with his cousin, Vizolet, and together, we've been setting out to fill a gap in the market: making ethically sourced and brilliantly effective beard products for men.

But our approach isn't just about men's grooming. We're also working to drive social change at the same time by addressing men's mental health issues, changing the dialogue around toxic masculinity, and working to dismantle patriarchal movements and mindsets. In 2018, we held a masterclass in which we addressed and discussed these issues with a panel of speakers, and, in 2019, Vizolet spoke about similar topics at another, related event. Our aim is nothing short of redefining what it means to be a man.

Refining and Redefining

TK has travelled all over Africa to source organic ingredients that provide comfort to the irritations of growing a beard, and the oils we use are carefully selected. Over the years, we've also taken the time to learn about the specific needs of our customers, and have steadily grown our customer base as a result. Our products are now available in five southern African countries, including South Africa, Zimbabwe, Namibia, Zambia and Malawi.

But our strategy has largely been carried in our heads and we're aware that communication, to some extent, hasn't always been our strong suit. During the course of 2019, we realised that we had a great concept, but that it wasn't being translated into a business as powerful and effective as it could be. In order to have a better shot at something meaningful, we started having some hard conversations about things that really matter in both our professional and personal lives.

And we started to refine a number of things, including some of the most important aspects of our business, such as our costing structure and oil formula. We knew that we had to make some serious changes in order to succeed.

Beards Under Lockdown

We weren't considered an essential service under South Africa's most stringent lockdown regulations and all of the raw materials we were importing came to a grinding halt. Our business stagnated. It felt like the whole world was on pause. But we soon realised that this period was an opportunity: it was the chance we needed to take a long, hard look at how to improve our business, how to manage our finances better, how to listen to our customers' needs, and ultimately how to improve their grooming experience.

TK used this time to do some economics e-learning, even though it isn't his favourite subject, and he listened to webinars on surviving a crisis, which he found inspirational. He also started investing his time in other causes that are meaningful to him, including volunteering at The Character Company, an organisation that mentors and supports young orphaned boys. The Character Company teaches the boys under their care important values and how to be better men in society, and TK's work involves encouraging them to take care of themselves, to care for and respect women, and to give back to their communities.

Vizolet used lockdown to slow down and reflect. He made an effort to stay fit and healthy and listened to podcasts on leadership, marketing and how to manage people better. His goal was to find new ways of serving his customers better and to learn how to be more intentional in his business affairs. Vizolet feels that global marketing trends are shifting towards a focus on humility and kindness, a trend that his brand believes in strongly.

Ready for the Future

Across the world and the continent, men are prioritising their appearance and investing in worthwhile products. With a beautifully designed and professional brand that instils confidence and trust in our customers, and with renewed focus in our future, we're ready to take our next, critical steps. Now more than ever, we're intent on providing sustainable products that address our customers' grooming needs, not only in Africa, but globally.

Covid-19 has taught us that there will always be storms along the way, but that these storms can be weathered. What matters is that you treat these challenges as opportunities, and emerge stronger (and better groomed) at the end of it all.

Message of Hope

"With renewed focus in our future, we're ready to take our next, critical steps."

Connect with us here www.brothersbeard.africa

Chapter 5

Think Forward

ADAPT OR DIE

Featuring:

- Andile Khumalo: I am an Entrepreneur

- Mark Sham: Suits & Sneakers

- Musa Kalenga: Brave Group

- Dan Stillerman: Excel Academy

"Hope is being able to see there is light despite all the darkness."
—Desmond Tutu

#ENTREPRENEURSSTAYALIVE
by Andile Khumalo

About Andile

> *Founder and CEO of family investment firm KhumaloCo, Andile Khumalo is a seasoned entrepreneur with 17 years of business experience. He is also the Founder of I AM AN ENTREPRENEUR and Chairman of Ince and the Brave Group. He serves as a fellow of The Centre for African Management and Markets at The Gordon Institute of Business Science and regularly writes on business and entrepreneurship as catalysts for real transformation. Visit iamanentrepreneur.co.za for #entrepreneursstayalive advice, inspiration and guidance.*

Love your Job

I come from a family of teachers and grew up in a township outside Durban, in fact our home was known as the 'staffroom' because almost all my aunts and uncles were teachers. As a young boy I was aware of my surroundings, which was very much a trading environment, and I was fascinated by the art of buying and selling. There was often violence in our neighbourhood and it was a pretty dark time, but once Nelson Mandela had been released, we knew something new was coming. There were opportunities for ambitious youth in the new South Africa and one of my high school teachers mentioned chartered accounting to me. I received a Deloitte bursary, qualified and travelled to Houston, Texas. Following a chance meeting with Khumo Shuenyane in a nightclub in Durban before a trip to the US, I joined Investec and found myself on a steep learning curve when I got back.

My plan has always been to create and build things, to be an entrepreneur, and I felt that I was in the right place at the right time.

I started my first business with friends and we raked in the public sector work, but I quickly realised that charging an hourly rate was not going to build real wealth. I then bought into a courier company, which we built up and sold. After that, I joined MSG Afrika, where we bought and built businesses, including a radio station from scratch, and had proved to myself that I could build things. But as I was approaching 40 I started thinking a lot about the life I wanted to live. I felt I could live a better life, the life I really wanted to live. I knew I had the ability and that the time was right. On Mandela Day in July 2018, I signed my exit agreement from MSG Afrika and started my family investment business, KhumaloCo, and also put time and energy into building I Am An Entrepreneur – a national programme that helps entrepreneurs grow their businesses (also known as "my love job").

Leaping into Action

On Saturday 14 March, our first IAAE summit of the year was due to kick off. We had heard rumours of Covid-19, but nobody expected what was about to unfold. On the Friday morning we had a quick meeting and realised we had two choices: either we ignore the warnings or we overreact. We decided to overreact. Overnight, we stocked up on hand sanitisers, found video content on how to wash your hands, had doctors on site at the summit and medical teams on standby. We even had a paramedic to screen people's temperatures, long before it became commonplace.

Entrepreneurs Stay Alive

I have a gift that I often take for granted, and that is I get over setbacks really quickly. I am not a moper. I analyse each angle, but I don't get hung up on the outcome. Since we have been forced into this new normal, we need to embrace digital and online platforms. We have started #entrepreneursstayalive, a series of interviews in which I talk to different entrepreneurs, industry leaders and heads of big corporates to dissect the effect and impact of Covid-19 on entrepreneurs and offer support, motivation and reasons to stay optimistic through this unprecedented time.

Agility is Everything

Most entrepreneurs have an emotional attachment to their business and although this is an important ingredient, businesses that survive any impact are those that understand the need to move quickly when it comes to change. You need to be honest and candid about the situation you find yourself in and, most importantly, ready to discover new avenues for revenue. It's as if you are starting a new business all over again, so you cannot be too attached to the old way of doing things. Agility is everything.

If you are an entrepreneur you are always looking for opportunities, and starting over means there are new skills you may need to learn or sharpen. Be inspired to think out-of-the box – in fact we may need to throw away the box we have been thinking out of, all these years. More often than not we are the weirdos, the crazy ones, and Covid-19 may just be the opportunity for more of us to come out of the woodwork. The world has been turned upside down and everything is up for discussion, people are listening, doors are opening. I am far more excited than I am depressed. The ray of hope is that the majority of mankind is working together to rescue this situation. Entrepreneurs have a zest for life and we will get through this.

Message of Hope

"People are listening, doors are opening – tune in."

Connect with us here https://iamanentrepreneur.co.za

ALWAYS MAKING A MARK
by Mark Sham

About Mark

Mark is an entrepreneur, writer and speaker who addresses audiences around the globe about being better prepared for the future. He is the founder and CEO of Suits & Sneakers, which has been in operation since 2015. He is also the founder of the Impello incubation hub. Mark is hell-bent on disrupting education for people of all ages in his attempt to make the world a better place.

The Power of an Informal Education

I was kicked out of school in my matric year and, as a result, didn't go to university. This event ultimately redirected the course of my life — not for the worse, as modern society would have you believe, but for the better. It was what taught me about the power of the internet, which allowed my endless curiosity to access similarly endless amounts of information.

The internet made me realise that going to university and coming out with a piece of a paper in hand belonged to an old and outdated system, and that this system could be hacked. The internet, I discovered, could give me an informal — but equally valuable — education instead. And so I threw myself into it head first and learnt all I possibly could.

Ultimately, I found myself at the head of a marketing business, but about five years ago, after a period of feeling quite lost, realised that I wanted more. I wanted to work closely with other people in order to help them become better versions of themselves. And so I sold my businesses and started Suits & Sneakers, an organisation designed to help people understand and harness the power of an informal education the way I had.

Today, Suits & Sneakers is an online learning management system and informal education hub, and our goal is to build a schooling system that gives young people free access to quality education. We're dismantling what was and creating something new and worthwhile in its place.

From London to Lockdown

I love travelling and regularly speak at events all over the world. In recent years, however, I started to look at my life holistically. The extent to which I was travelling wasn't sustainable and I realised that I needed to create a business that allowed me to work from anywhere at any time. My business model has historically involved me physically being in various places, and only has a very small digital component.

In January 2019, I moved to London, partly for the hustle and bustle I so love, and partly because I found that, from there, I could start to implement my new business model with ease. And when I did need to travel, I felt like I was centrally located between South Africa and other parts of the world I regularly visit. By February 2020, I was really starting to enjoy the benefits of a more balanced lifestyle.

And then came Covid-19.

Within 72 hours, my world turned on its head: all of my future revenue was cancelled and I had to make the urgent decision to stay in London or come back to South Africa. I decided to come back home: to better weather, to my friends and family, and to where I wouldn't have to isolate alone. But the experience was gutting. Just when I felt like I was finally getting it all right, I had had to leave behind a business model that I had worked so hard on. The carpet had been swept out from underneath me completely.

And as I considered my various options, I found myself reluctant to move my events online, as so many other businesses were doing. I love interacting with people; for me it's all about the face to face.

The Value of Going Digital

As the days of lockdown unfolded, I remembered a guiding principle that has always helped me during troubled times: the importance of helping other people. It's been my strategy for years and has defined my business model and work ethic. As soon as you look beyond yourself, you're destined for success. I looked at my Facebook page and its large following, and realised that I could use it to my advantage.

I started hosting webinars, primarily on issues relating to mental health, and promoted these through Facebook. I was over the moon when I sold my first webinar: it was just so satisfying to be earning a little bit of money again. But I soon realised that it wasn't about the money, it was about adding value — and that spurred me on even more.

Transferring my events to the digital world, I soon learnt, had its benefits. Webinars allow me to engage with thousands of people at any given point in time, and if people can't attend in the moment, they can watch a recording of it in their own time via social media. Live events, of course, can't do this. My early lockdown webinars have led me to speaking at other digital events, to setting up a video and podcasting studio in the heart of Sandton, and to creating more content and hosting more webinars. It's been so exciting that Covid-19 might have single-handedly been the greatest thing to ever happen to my business.

Pain and Growth

This isn't to suggest that it's all been easy — it's certainly been painful and difficult at times too. But if I've learnt anything, it's that pain is a precursor for growth. And growth is certainly on the cards.

I've realised that if I want to scale this business, the way forward is a hybrid between the digital and the face to face. I'm therefore in the process of creating several webinar series for many different companies, and for Suits & Sneakers too. And in many ways, I feel like I'm going back to my roots: a lot of my sessions involve teaching people about the massive and overwhelming opportunities that the digital world affords us.

I'm teaching people about digital destruction. Mike Tyson famously said, "Everybody has a plan until you get punched in the face." Covid-19 has punched us in the face — hard — but it's up to us to capitalise on this opportunity, to reach a point of acceptance, and to make meaningful, conscious decisions that will benefit us in the long term.

At the same time, I'm using my platforms to discuss other issues that are important to me: the importance of our attitude and mindset, for example, and how much our perspective on things can affect how we interpret and interact with the world. My webinars are designed to help people look at these important points.

Excited, Happy and Hopeful

In a bold move, I recently pitched a free series of five webinar episodes to Amazon. The topics ranged from getting your mental game back on track, to leading in uncertain times, and discussions on the hybrid model of remote working. I emphasised the importance of subtle marketing in my pitch and the need to help people during this crisis. When Amazon bit, I couldn't believe it — it was just the most incredible moment and a real validation of the work I've been doing. Our first few episodes had over 10,000 attendees.

I have never been more encouraged and optimistic about my business and have learnt two important lessons during this time: the first is not to pay attention to the negative opinion of others. You simply can't give a fuck. The second is to practise empathy. You've got to show your vulnerability, connect to the vulnerability in others, and be authentic. Now, more than ever, people can see through the bull, and they're not interested in cute and fluffy offerings that mean nothing. Consumers want to know what's in it for them, and if you can prove that you're able to help them, that you're a fighter for collective action and that you're living with purpose, you're likely to create allies.

Managing Expectations and Cultivating Hope

Increasingly, I myself focusing on the importance of having our actions and decisions come from the heart, and I'm trying to help people better understand how they feel and think about their happiness.

One of my favourite quotes is: "Expectation is simply the agreement you make with yourself that you won't be happy unless you get what you want." Part of the reason why I was so upset about how 2020 began is because there was a disconnect between my expectations and the reality. But, as it turned out, the new, unexpected reality has been better than I could have ever imagined.

The human spirit thrives: somehow, it picks itself up and moves on. A critical part of this is hope. Hope helps us to move forward, and inspires us to create value and build something more meaningful than what existed before.

Message of Hope

"Covid-19 might have single-handedly been the greatest thing to ever happen to my business."

Connect with Mark here http://suitsandsneakers.co.za and like his page SA Citizens Unite or follow the hashtag #SACitizensUnite to see what his up to.

BE THE CHANGE
by Musa Kalenga

About Musa

> *A passionate serial entrepreneur, Musa Kalenga is CEO and Founder of Bridge Labs, which addresses the problem of gaining access to appropriate online tools for entrepreneurs and Small to Medium Businesses by building mobile platforms to support growth in emerging markets. He also holds the position of Chief Future Officer at House of Brave, a creative advertising agency. As a respected thought leader in the marketing industry, Musa advises on digital marketing strategy for businesses with his Marketing in a Digital World Executive Programme. His most important role, however, is father to two young children.*

A Punch in the Face

Covid-19 has been a punch in the face for entrepreneurs. It's a challenging time for small businesses: we have to go back to the drawing board and rapidly create, plan and execute as flawlessly as possible. Overnight, we have had to take care of our business and immediate staff, being mindful to keep them not only physically safe, but psychologically safe as well, giving them reasons to feel optimistic about the future. Our immediate network of staff need to feel taken care of with regards to this virus. Before lockdown, much of my time was taken up with public speaking, and this crisis has forced me to shift my world.

Synaptic Shake-Up

The estate that my family and I live on was put into lockdown a week before the rest of the country due to the fact that one of the residents had contracted Covid-19. For the first time, I had to take a new look at our family home and become more involved in the daily lives of my children. I had to deal with a range of emotions regarding their education, which had me engaging and stimulating different neural pathways. When you have your back against the wall, proficiency leads to a sleepy brain. When you do the same process over and over, you make your brain lazy, but by doing things differently it jolts your grey matter and this has got me thinking again: I had to do something fundamentally different since I am ultimately responsible not only for my own future but for the future of my family, and together we have put some new systems in place.

Journal Insights

One of the first things I did when lockdown began was revisit the journals I have kept over the years. I'm the kind of guy that talks about change all the time and to keep myself inspired, I kept journals – this has been a discipline of mine for a long time and each year I choose a journal in a different colour to keep track of the journey I have been on. It was fascinating to be reminded of things that had happened in the past. This was a cathartic exercise and it helped me to realise that, as individuals, we can achieve a lot through adversity. Sentences like these were dotted all over the place: "I don't know how I'm going to make it through", "I don't know how we are going to pay salaries..."

My journals helped me to take stock and despite feeling like my back was against the wall, I know that a lot of good can and does happen through adversity.

Strategic Thinking Toolkit

I have tried as much as possible to talk to entrepreneurs and young people at this time – I find it invigorating to share. I came up with a model I call 'Adaptnation' and started sharing this with a lot of small businesses. It involves diagnosing, making peace with, and crafting a new journey for your organisation. For a lot of companies, thinking strategically about what to do next doesn't come naturally. I have put together a toolkit to help small businesses generate a strategy to work through.

There are four essential components:

- Stabilization of the business
- Assessing opportunity
- Pivoting
- Growth acceleration

Our intention is to proof test this model and then make it widely available to entrepreneurs; when they work through the process, they generate data. It is effectively a trusted advisor for small businesses, a toolkit to address leadership, middle management, processes and technology.

Communication is Key

People have been desk bound and are now working from home – this can be a weird space for many, so good communication is essential. Some may be all alone in a flat, some may be surrounded by a busy family and others may not have an appropriate work space in their home. The 'fancy' corporate office space is now obsolete and, operationally, we are changing businesses to be more data driven.

I would like to lead with understanding and intelligence, and double down on our service proposition. I have looked back in order to look forward and work differently. Through the use of technology, the invisible digital economy will be able to create viable, affordable and sustainable solutions that will solve crucial problems in our society.

Lessons Learnt

My advice to other entrepreneurs is to reflect on "what is the worst that could happen?" You need to trust your intuition and make the necessary changes to survive. Appreciate that it's a new chapter for us all. Begin with something small and work your way towards some fundamental shifts in how you do business.

Human beings are more resilient than we give ourselves credit for. We will persevere and we will survive if we shift and adapt. There will be a number of casualties along the way, but just don't forget to turn. A sharp bend in the road is only dangerous if you forget to turn.

Message of Hope

"A lot of good can and does happen through adversity."

Connect with Musa here www.kalenga.me

FORMULA OF EXCEL-LENCE
by Dan Stillerman

About Dan

> *Dan Stillerman founded Excel Academy in 2014. This came after four years of working as an actuary, and pushing Excel to the limits. Excel Academy has established a reputation as a global leader in improving productivity and success in the workplace.*
>
> *To date, the team has positively influenced the lives of over 20,000 people through their unique and fun approach and blended learning model. Over the years, the content has been focused primarily on Excel, but since the beginning of the Covid-19 pandemic, Dan and his team have evolved their offering, and now help people to use programmes such as Zoom, PowerPoint and Outlook with confidence and success.*
>
> *Dan is an avid runner, a proud South African, and a respected thought leader in the South African Jewish community.*

A Quarter-Life Crisis

Between 2009 and 2013, I worked as an actuary at a start-up life insurer, where my role was almost completely focused on Excel. In my first few months on the job, I found Excel overwhelming and confusing, and often felt like I wasn't adding much value. I even thought I was going to be fired! But as time wore on, I learnt more and more, and my confidence started to grow. It's amazing what you can do with a tool like Excel when you start to unlock its potential.

In September 2013, the day after I qualified as an actuary, I quit my job. I had always believed that I would work my way up the corporate ladder and be successful and happy, but around that time, at the age of 26, I started asking myself, "Am I in the right environment? Is this the right vehicle for me to achieve the impact I want to achieve? Am I happy?"

Perhaps you could call it a quarter-life crisis. I realised there was more to life than what I was currently doing, and I started to wonder what people needed and how I could help. I went on a number of personal development courses, many of which were on entrepreneurship, and I started to discover and develop a passion for helping people, for building brands, and for making an impact in the world.

Excel Academy

And so I founded Excel Academy. The goal? To help people to become more confident, productive and successful in their lives and businesses by leveraging the power of Excel. In the early stages, my business model involved face-to-face workshops, which I conducted on-site at clients. I created three workshops, Excel 101, Excel 202 and Excel 303, and structured them as a learning journey that was designed to build students' confidence, curiosity and skillset through an interactive, fun and stimulating learning experience.

After two years, I realised that there were limitations to the in-person business model. I could only be in one physical space at a time, and eight-hour training workshops are exhausting for the trainer and delegates alike. I started to train up a few other trainers, but the model was still scalable only in a linear way, and I also had the challenge of ensuring that my new trainers were meeting the high standards I had set.

With a goal of reaching more and more people, I started to transform the training from face-to-face workshops to an online learning experience. The other trainers and I recorded ourselves and our Excel screens, and made every effort to replicate the fun, interactive nature of the classroom experience.

The Online Shift

Over the last few years, we've realised that there are certain crucial elements that we need to incorporate in order to maximise the engagement and success of the training. One is the introduction of onboarding or kick-starting sessions, which are either run in person or via a Zoom webinar. These sessions provide us with the opportunity to introduce delegates to the training, to walk them through the online platform so they feel comfortable and confident to navigate it themselves, to answer their questions, and to ensure that they buy into the experience and commit to completing the training within a certain time frame.

We provide high-touch support to our delegates, incentives for successful completion, and lifetime access to the courses. Our clients love the fact that they can work through the content in their own time and at their own pace.

Our unique gamified and blended approach has resulted in a more effective, flexible, cost-efficient and scalable training solution for organisations. It's also allowed us to reach tens of thousands of people around South Africa and the rest of the world. We're especially proud of our completion rates, which are consistently over 95%.

Stepping up as a Leader

At the beginning of March, I started to feel a heightened sense of fear and uncertainty as the pandemic began to escalate and the nationwide lockdown loomed. I realised that there was going to be a sudden need for people to connect via Zoom. On the eve of lockdown, I walked into a coffee shop and ran into a friend. During our conversation, I mentioned that I was thinking of running free training sessions on how to use Zoom. His immediate reaction was, " Do it! This is your time to shine!" I realised that this was a pivotal opportunity for me to step up as a leader, and that I was in a unique position to make a real difference.

On 17 March, I ran a free webinar called "How to Teach Via Webinar" and was blown away by the number of questions I received and the enormous interest that was generated. We had just over 200 people on that webinar, and probably over 200 questions. Afterwards, I got a call from the Union of Jewish Women to host a webinar on the potential medical and financial impact of Covid-19. Then the SA Jewish Report newspaper contacted me with the idea to host a medical Q&A webinar with some of South Africa's top healthcare professionals. Over 1,000 people watched live and thousands more watched the recording. We had people tuning in from all over the world who were grateful for the critical information we were providing for free.

Webinars give us the opportunity to help people by providing information, entertainment, connection and engagement, all of which are essential during these uncertain, difficult, and often lonely and isolating times. We have received so much genuine appreciation from people near and far. I recently spoke to an elderly South African woman who has been alone in her flat in Los Angeles for three months, and who told me that our webinars provide her with a sense of connection and belonging. She's tuned in to just about every webinar, and she shares them with all her friends.

Up and Up

As at 11 June 2020 – day 77 of lockdown in South Africa – we had hosted over 120 webinars. One of the most unique and memorable webinar was South Africa's first online art auction for charity, which was a deeply fulfilling and inspiring experience. We raised over R2 million for the Solidarity Fund and the Vulnerable Artist Fund.

We have also hosted "Lockdown's Got Talent", "Kick-starting the South African Economy", and interviews with industry experts and thought leaders such as Adrian Gore, Herman Mashaba and Solly Krok. We've covered topics such as maintaining one's physical and mental wellness during this time and the new world of work; facilitated debates on whether children should go back to school; and hosted cooking and baking shows, a general knowledge quiz, an "Amazing Race", and several other fascinating panel discussions and forums.

We're finding more and more demand from businesses who are wanting to use our platform and expertise to host their webinars, and we're now including this service in our offering.

Clarity and Purpose

Amid what feels like a tsunami of uncertainty, anxiety and stress – and unrelenting phone calls, Zoom sessions and emails – I have done my best to maintain a balance and stay fit, healthy and well rested.

We have grown our database significantly during this time, and it's been an opportunity to expand our brand and positioning in our community and in the market in general. I feel inspired to continue this important work. I feel that this is a time to be generous, understanding and kind, and not to focus too much on profit. It's about maintaining a big picture outlook and focusing on building, maintaining and strengthening relationships with clients. Now is the time to show people that you genuinely care.

What has really stood us in good stead is being crystal clear about why we are in business. We believe that business is about helping people. Making money is a result. A strong sense of purpose has been critical to me and to our business, and encouraging other businesses to find their purpose is the best piece of advice I can offer.

Having a sense of purpose will guide you and your team and will provide you with clarity and direction, even during the most challenging of times. I'm well aware that the challenges many people and businesses are facing right now are unprecedented. But even so, I do believe that having clarity of purpose, and finding creative ways to bring that purpose to life, will do wonders for one's resilience, and one's ability to stay in business and thrive in the future.

Message of Hope

"I started to wonder what people needed and how I could help."

Connect with us here https://www.excelacademyinc.com/

Chapter 6

Courage

TRIUMPH OVER ADVERSITY

Featuring:

- Kate Shepherd: Something Different

- Renshia Manuel: Growbox

- Dr Angelique Marie Levy Oliveira

- Alison McCutcheon: Ladles of Love

"Once you choose hope, anything is possible."
– *Christopher Reeve*

PHOENIX RISING
by Kate Shepherd

About Kate

> *Kate Shepherd is the founding owner of design businesses Something Different, Something Desired and Something Designed, which are based in both Cape Town and Johannesburg.*
>
> *Something Different is a design and build business that works in any environment, including homes, offices, and shopping and recreational spaces, and offers a comprehensive solution from concept development through to execution.*
>
> *Kate was a finalist for Regional Entrepreneur of the Year in 2016, and has been featured on many TV programmes, blogs and magazines. She is often invited to comment on décor, design and creative trends in interior spaces, and to offer insight on being an entrepreneur. She has been identified as "one of the top 15 women in South Africa to know" and as "one of South Africa's top seven inspiring wonder women" by Woman & Home.*

Something Different

Something Different was born when I was just 18 years old and, in the years since, we have grown from a home office and a garage for storage, to large warehouses filled to the brim in multiple cities. This growth has been deeply humbling – and exciting – to witness.

Something Different's core function is spatial design: we both create new environments and transform existing spaces. We put this into practice in everything from events and activations, to home interiors and office design. We thrive in dreaming up ideas and making them a reality.

Making Impossible Decisions

In January 2020, my business was doing really well – it was in the midst of its best year ever, in fact. It had always been my dream to launch in the UK and I started this process by registering the Something Different business name in London.

February brought with it rumblings about the virus, and despite initially believing that it was happening elsewhere, we soon started to feel its impact. Almost overnight, corporates started pulling back and every project and event that was scheduled for February was either postponed or cancelled. But we'd survived the global recession in 2008, the water crisis in Cape Town and repeated bouts of load shedding, surely this wasn't going to be any different? Unfortunately, it was. In no time at all, we were reeling. Within 10 days, our income had dropped to zero.

I turned to my American business coach, and asked what he had regretted in previous crises. He said that, after September 11, he had regretted not moving fast enough. "If there is a decision to be made, make it now," he said. My UK business advisors said the same thing: act swiftly, it will be more painful in the short term but it will also give you more time to recover. I probably would have hesitated and damaged my business further had it not been for these conversations.

I went to see a lawyer and running through the many options she gave me most viable was to shut my business down quickly. This would give my staff the chance to be among the first to apply for UIF, she said, as well as get more out of the liquidation. Lockdown had not been enforced yet, but I knew that, once it was, things would only get worse. I wanted to make sure that my staff would have the best opportunity to get back on their feet, even though letting them down was the most difficult thing I've ever had to do.

After 15 years of a successful and fulfilling business, I made the difficult decision to close Something Different permanently. To say I was heartbroken is an understatement.

17 March 2020

I'll never forget 17 March. It was the hardest day of my life. I called a crisis meeting and although some of the staff had been told that this meeting could be more serious than they anticipated, many were saying, "Whatever's going on is Kate's problem, not ours". I don't think anyone quite believed that the virus would have this sort of impact, and that we would have gone from thriving to dead in less than 10 days.

But the situation had affected my business so seriously that I had to tell 40 people that I didn't have enough money to survive this, and that they no longer had a job. The experience was incredibly emotional for me – and for everyone there. Some were crying, and two or three stormed out of the room and didn't want to listen to the solutions or suggestions I had.

The higher end staff criticised me for not including them in the decision-making process. (In hindsight, this was the right choice. It was not for them to make this terrible decision; the burden was on me as the owner.) The lower income staff took the business closure better; some were thankful, humble and kind. That day, I had to repeat the devastating news over and over. I had to tell our Johannesburg staff, any others not present, and I had to write to all our clients and suppliers.

After this I had to endure weeks of hell. I was trolled online and my personal character attacked. The negativity and resentment was extreme. I became a punching bag for everybody. It was so hard to see people turn on me; I was horrified that they thought of me as a monster. To date, the online abuse, lawsuits and CCMA cases haven't stopped, despite there being no grounds. Defending myself against this constant attack has been truly exhausting.

Blow by Blow

At the end of March, South Africa went into lockdown. At home, I tackled mountains of paperwork: UIF forms, creditor and lawyer documents, and client correspondence. I also had to fight for payments – the decision to close my business, after all, brought with it significant financial pressures. I found it really hard to function, and being strong for my children was a daily struggle. I have a two year old and a five year old and had to hide my emotions when they were around. In those first few days, I often had to take myself off to the bathroom to have a good cry. I felt devastated and completely lost.

We are a close family and, on top of everything, my mom was admitted to hospital for a kidney infection in the UK around this time. My dad caught Covid-19 shortly after, and spent 20 days bedridden in isolation, away from my mom who had just got out of hospital and was high risk. My brother, an NHS doctor, also contracted the virus, and my grandmother fell and broke her hip. It felt like my entire life was crumbling around me. That's when survival mode kicked in.

Survival Mode

One night shortly into lockdown, my husband, mother-in-law and I — all of whom had lost our income — sat down to choose an essential service that we could support. My mother-in-law can sew and so we decided to produce face masks. We started off small, producing 20 to 30 a day and selling them to the people in our road. We then ramped up to between 50 and 80 a day, before starting to use more fashionable fabrics and connecting to seamstresses working in impoverished communities.

Thanks to these incredible people we are now able to produce up to 100,000 masks, and are pushing out hundreds every week. For every 100 masks we make, we donate 10 to essential workers on the frontlines and to various NGOs and soup kitchens. For us, simply creating the means for people to protect themselves wasn't enough, we also wanted to give back and support others. These efforts, and knowing that we are making a difference, have eased the pain I have felt during this time.

From Failure to Flourishing

At the moment, I feel guilty that I have hustled hard enough to make enough money to put food on the table and pay our bills. But this new venture isn't about making large amounts of money; it's about being useful during this crisis. And for that, I feel proud. Last month I was able to make enough to send some of my staff food parcels. In addition, a local school has asked me to host some webinars and it's reassuring to know my experience and knowledge is still worth something; it's helping me to get my confidence back.

Making masks isn't going to be my career forever, but it has made me realise I have what it takes to start anew. I've come to understand that, although it felt like it, Something Different didn't define me, I am who I am outside of being its owner. I've realised that I can make something from a piece of cloth and that being an entrepreneur is part of who I am.

Message of Hope

"The experience has helped me believe that I, like the Phoenix, which is the symbol of strength and renewal, can move from failure to flourishing, even in the darkest of times and rise again."

Connect with Kate here www.superheroeswearmasks.co.za or drop her an email at hello@rebelcollective.co

DIG DEEP
by Renshia Manuel

About Renshia

Renshia Manuel is the passionate founder and managing director of GrowBox Wholesale Nursery, and lives by her company's tagline: #JustKeepGrowing. She has participated in several social entrepreneur programmes and competitions including:

- #YouthStartCT Entrepreneurial challenge 2016: 3ʳᵈ place
- Raizcorp Engen Pitch n Polish 2017: 3ʳᵈ place
- Awief Growth Accelerator 2018: 3ʳᵈ place
- Samsung Global Startup Accelerator 2018: 2ⁿᵈ place (as well as SA Ambassador to Samsung Head Office in Seoul, South Korea)
- Finalist in the Inco Women Entrepreneur of the Year 2019
- Winner of the Santam Fairlady Women of the Future Awards in the Social Entrepreneurship Category 2019

Sewing the Seeds of Hope

My journey started in 2015. I was unemployed and struggling to feed my four children, so I transformed a dead, vacant space in my backyard in Hanover Park into a vegetable garden that had us eating from it for months. My kids were so excited, because I'd let them decide what we would eat, and it was their duty to harvest our dinner from the garden.

In 2016 I saw an ad in the local paper for a competition, #YouthStartCT Entrepreneurial Challenge, that invited unemployed youth to submit sustainable business ideas that would uplift the communities in which they operate. It was then that I had the idea of opening a wholesale nursery in Hanover Park.

Entrants attended workshops at Cape Town civic centre that helped us with our pitches, presentations and how to hone our social impact; we were encouraged to "find our niche" – in other words, identify or formulate what sets us apart from our competitors.

I began to wonder what could set me apart from other wholesale nurseries, but also be beneficial to communities like the one I come from. How could I help low-income households with limited space to grow their own food?

The answer was GrowBox – that's how my company started. We manufacture wooden planter boxes fully stocked with vegetable seedlings to sell to our community. Our aim is to increase food security within disadvantaged households by manufacturing these veggie boxes for individuals to grow vegetables in small or limited spaces around their homes. We also source seedlings wholesale and sell these on to retail nurseries, government entities and the public, and we offer training and skills development.

Working Out the Box

In the first two weeks of lockdown, we took a huge knock and it was difficult to work out a way forward. All I did initially was focus on planting, growing and building up our stock. For security reasons, I had to move all the stock from the Hanover Park nursery to our home. We put up makeshift shelves, so the plants were everywhere – there wasn't even space for our dogs to lie down!

During Level 5 of lockdown, essential services were allowed to operate and I used this opportunity to apply for a permit so that we could service the farmers. Once we went to Level 4, the horticultural services could continue and we could move the plants back to the nursery. But first we had to sanitise the premises and make sure we were hygiene compliant to reassure our clients and put them at ease. Hanover Park has a huge stigma attached to it, it is gang territory, and our community is very cautious so we have had to work hard to give our clients peace of mind. In the initial stages of lockdown, there was a huge demand as people needed access to food, but we couldn't do any foodscaping as our clients were afraid of us working in their gardens.

We did a lot of GrowBox deliveries though, and we realised that, as a collective, people were seeing how impactful growing their own food could be. Given that food is so expensive, they could see the value of harvesting food from their own garden — so lockdown, for us, can be seen as a blessing.

This too, Shall Pass

My business has already had two crises before this one. The first was the drought in Cape Town, which devastated our crops. The second was being robbed just as I was getting GrowBox up and running. Everything was stolen: from our seedlings to our water pumps, equipment and damages to structures and fencing, we were cleaned out. So this is my third crisis. I have four children depending on me to dig deep and find solutions. Thankfully I have an amazing group of people supporting me. Mentors, friends and business associates who check up on me and help me to stay positive.

The Courage to do Things Differently

One of my personal challenges is that I used to be an introvert and my confidence and self-worth wasn't great. I would often think that what I'm doing isn't good enough. But I have been blessed with opportunities and although it has taken me a long time I can now ask for help. Being an island doesn't get you anywhere. I know that it might sound like a cliché, but I did not choose agriculture — it chose me. Do not let anyone ever convince you that you cannot overcome an obstacle. The solution might not be clear at first, but sooner or later it will be.

My lesson through all of this has been to be flexible. No one could have predicted that this catastrophe would occur. We have had to work around certain things, figure out ways around the restrictions and not become stagnant. I coped by keeping busy: I grew seedlings, supplied to growers and my intention is to expand GrowBox into a gardening programme next to the Hanover Park nursery so that the community can grow their own vegetables there and sell them at a food market. We would like to roll this market out to the Cape Flats by employing community members to run the business, so that they can achieve economic freedom by supplying food directly to the market. The social grant system won't sustain families; they need to be self-sufficient.

I've challenged myself to improve my time management and embrace new on-line platforms like Zoom and online social media postings, but most importantly, become self-sufficient so that I can empower my community to do the same.

Find your Guiding Light

My message of hope to other social entrepreneurs is to decide on your core values, find the need in your community and find a solution to that need. Use this as a guiding light. My core values are to leave a legacy for my family and my community, and to keep advocating food sovereignty for all. Lockdown has highlighted the true need in our communities, and that is economic empowerment. We need to provide skills and support for them to get out of the poverty cycle. GrowBox can give them a boost, encourage them to think differently and to take action.

Message of Hope

"Lockdown has highlighted the need for economic empowerment."

Connect with us here http://www.growboxnursery.com

NOT ALL ANGELS HAVE WINGS
by Dr Angelique Marie Levy Oliveira

About Dr Angelique Oliveira

Dr. Angelique M. Oliveira is the CEO and Founder of In-Harmony, a successful wellness consultancy that specialises in maximizing human potential, by conducting assessments and then developing unique strategies, products, services and solutions that improve health, happiness, and success. She completed her Bachelor of Medicine and Surgery at the University of the Witwatersrand in 2018, at 37 she is currently in her second year of internship at Groote Schuur Hospital in Cape Town.

The Move to Medicine

All I can say is, I'm exhausted. I work in one of the Covid-19 units at Groote Schuur Hospital in Cape Town, and at times the experience has been nothing short of challenging. Everyday the global medical community share the latest research in the fight against this disease, which is like nothing I've seen before.

My childhood dream was to become a doctor, but I did a number of things before studying medicine, including working as a computer programmer, studying an honours in psychology at Stellenbosch University, and starting a corporate wellness company. After overcoming a few obstacles, I decided to tackle medicine.

I believe that Groote Schuur is the best hospital in South Africa; I love the working environment and the friendliness of the staff. They go above and beyond to ensure that all staff are safe and that patients receive the very best care.

January, February and March

In January and February 2020, I was working in the hospital's trauma unit, which provides care for patients suffering from injuries caused by falls, motor vehicle accidents, and gunshot or stab wounds. But by March, I had moved to the endocrine surgery unit where I was fortunate enough to be under the leadership of Prof. Lydia Cairncross. Not only is she a phenomenal surgeon but also a defender of human rights.

When Covid-19 reached pandemic status the hospital was already planning and preparing for it before it hit the hospital. Prof. Cairncross and the team advocated for increasing surgeries for urgent cancer patients before the hospital would be forced to cut back on all surgical procedures. Patients who need endocrine surgery include those who suffer from breast and thyroid cancer, among others. Unfortunately, Covid-19 cancer patients are at higher risk of mortality so the push was on to increase our team's surgeries while other nonessential surgeries cut back and eventually stopped altogether. It was intense but rewarding.

Covid-19, Doing the Rounds

Near the beginning of March the hospital got its first Covid-19-positive case. It felt like we were all holding our breath. As interns, we are sheltered from some of the decisions taking place behind management doors, but our professor having an open relationship with us, allowed us to voice our concerns. We all felt informed and heard.

The atmosphere in the hospital changed when we were faced with the first fatality, but the reality set in when hospital staff became patients and then sadly fatalities.

In those early days, there was a lot of misinformation going around with media outlets polarised between the views of this being 'just like the flu' versus this being one of the deadliest virus we've seen. Fortunately, I had access to medical journals and our hospitals statistics, but it was evident that this virus was unique and necessitated a global medical collaboration for sharing of information and experiences.

One of the most surprising things for me was the fact that people could have very low pulse oximeter readings and show no clinical signs of such hypoxaemia. A pulse oximeter reading measures how much oxygen is in the blood a low reading (hypoxaemia) can lead to hypoxia which refers to a deficiency in the amount of oxygen reaching the tissues. Healthy people have oxygen saturation levels of around 98% - 99% and should be above 94%. This was the first time I've seen people with readings below 50% and still able to talk - saying they actually feel fine. Hypoxaemia is dangerous and can result in damage to vital organs in the body, often the lower the level the poorer the outcome. One of the other surprising factors was that the virus seems to cause not only respiratory cell damage but also endothelial and nerve cell damage. As is evidenced by the way it's able to cause blood clots and damage the sense of smell.

The Frontline

I then moved to the Internal Medicine department, which deals with the prevention, diagnosis, and treatment of internal diseases, one of which is pneumonia. I knew I would be dealing with Covid-19 and that I was now at the frontline of the crisis.

There was a Covid-19 team managing all the Covid-19 wards but as the numbers increased the hospital ran out of space on the floor that was designated for Covid-19. So, the hospital had to make space on the general medicine floor and the team I was in, was responsible for the Covid-19 wards on that floor.

Every morning we would get all the latest statistics, scrub up, and put on our full personal protective equipment. Our small group managed two wards one PUI (people under investigation, that is, people suspected of having Covid-19 but awaiting their results) and a Covid-19 positive ward.

We had to be absolutely vigilant not only when dealing with patients but also everywhere in the ward so that we didn't contaminate the areas in which we were working. Navigating this space was extremely stressful and emotionally taxing.

The first night our Covid-19 positive ward opened four people passed away. The loss of a patient is an impossible weight to carry but I find it a hard weight to put down, I cried a lot. The situation was unique in that we would be calling family members daily, to update them on their loved ones. So, when we had to break the news of their passing it was especially hard. The hardest thing for me was watching people die alone and afraid. It pushed me to form brief moments of human connection over and above being their doctor. However, I'd find myself wondering if I did enough, researched enough or what else we could be doing to help these patients.

Of course, we've also had many recoveries. I'll never forget the day one of my patients: an old lady with many co-morbidities – that made it seem like she would never recover – sat up with a huge smile and eventually recovered well enough for us to send her home. The whole ward doctors, nurses, cleaning staff all cheered as she left. We celebrated moments like these because they uplifted our whole unit, they are a win for all of us. It's a really beautiful feeling to ease someone else's pain and see them getting better.

Facing Reality

On a personal level, I have found the reality of this situation really difficult. Not being connected socially; myself and my patients to their families makes this more difficult – while necessary to help curb the spread of the virus.

I'm not sleeping very well and haven't got a lot of free time to FaceTime my friends and family, and of course I'm not seeing them in person. I live alone and am not very good at taking care of myself – I tend to bury myself in research. The emotional toll this experience is taking on me and the pace at which everything is happening is just exhausting. Nothing fully prepares you for this.

That said, I am processing and reflecting on what I am facing, and I am taking the time to sit with my feelings. Constantly thinking about work is draining and I realise I need to make time for myself, find balance, make an effort to sleep more and not be so hard on myself.

Message of Hope

"My message of hope is this: In such tumultuous times gratitude is vital. Taking moments to breathe, and to be grateful for that breath never seemed more relevant. Don't listen to the media hype or anticipate worst-case scenarios. Stay in the present moment and find fulfilment within it, uncontaminated by

negativity. Remember that we are all essentially just walking each other home so let's care for each other along the way. We have to find ways to connect virtually, to show care and compassion, and to be kind to one another. It's only through thinking about, supporting and uplifting others that we are able to put our own problems into perspective."

"Stop looking outside for scraps of pleasure or fulfillment, for validation, security, or love - you have a treasure that is infinitely greater than anything the world can offer."

– Eckhart Tolle

Connect with Dr Angelique M. Oliveira here https://www.linkedin.com/in/ angeliqueoliveira/

ISOLATION REALISATION
by Ali McCutcheon

About Ali

> *Born and bred in Cape Town, Alison was the product of parents who provided her with a fortunate and fantastic childhood. Her love for writing, reading and early adopting of the ethos of ubuntu, comes from her mother Jean Lowe, a wise, educated and travelled woman raised in the Eastern Cape -fluent in Xhosa and with a real connection to the people. From her father, Peter Lowe, came her confidence, gregarious nature, sense of humour and business mindedness. Her schooling and education was limited through health and learning challenges, so it was her curiosity, inquisitive mind, short marketing courses, learning multiple jobs and career in magazines that gave her the courage to start her own business. Selective Media and Promotions was launched in 1988 which then morphed into Rainbow Productions/ Experiential Marketing in 1994.*

A Brief Overview

My story starts in 2019 when my company, Rainbow Experiential Marketing, which was established in 1994 post-election, began to take enormous strain. The impact of the deteriorating economy was taking its toll on the marketing and event industry and the projects that ordinarily would roll-in starting drying up or worse still, after months and months of research and development as pre-investment – were cancelled.

After hours of internal discussions and dissecting each scenario we figured out the why? It was not our offering as we are agile and constantly re-invent ourselves, it was simply the ripple effect of a crippled economy's impact on our clients and their customers.

So we had to take swift action as the writing was on the wall and one thing being in business for decades give you is hindsight! If we do not learn from our lessons and act, immediately we will be doomed.

When you make serious decisions like this it impacts you both emotionally, physically and financially so by the end of 2019 I got the worst bout of bronchitis and had to take time out. This gave me time to re-group, re-calibrate and gather my grit for the New Year.

Tipping Rainbows into Ladles

I entered 2020 gingerly, without any expectations of anything at all and threw myself into my writing trying to find solace for my terror of facing a year of uncertainty and lack of financial stability. I found peace and calm and decided to explore a 'side hustle' mentoring people who could learn from my over three decades as a business owner. Meanwhile Rainbow was ticking over with requests for quotations and proposals flowing through the door — all unpaid work and on three, sometime five way pitches. The reality was, our chances were slim at best.

Out of the blue we started winning pitches and securing business, life was looking hopeful and I shifted from thinking we had passed our sell-by date as a company, to thinking my son, Matt Mulhall, who is has been a Director of Rainbow for four years now — just might have a business to be proud of. Then when we retire, I together with my business partner, Debbie McGuire would have a lasting legacy!

Enter March when I was in Gauteng on business feeling chipper and full of the joys of spring, the Coronavirus had barely hit our shores but by no means was a threat, so life was good. I am standing in a meeting with a blue-chip client when I can see someone is desperately trying to get hold of me! That call was the beginning of scores more — every event we had booked for 2020 was cancelled, one after the other. My forward book was bare and life had changed in that moment — irrevocably. Rainbow went from experiential marketers to packing of ten thousand hygiene parcels for one of our clients, which we were so grateful for, as we were desperately trying to stem the financially blood bath. And so our Covid-19 journey to more purpose-driven work began and as we wound down our hygiene packing project I reached out to one of our NPO clients, Danny Diliberto, founder of Ladles of Love, to say I am here to help — pro bono!

Currency of Kindness

During my rock and roll years of staging and produce live music concerts, I met my current husband, Les McCutcheon, who is a London based record company owner. For decades he has commuted to Cape Town and back. Our home is here but his business is there. When the UK joined the Coronavirus carnage my Groom was stuck in London – the thought of him in lockdown on his own a million miles away in a hotel room was a nightmare. After endless calls we eventually got him home on the last SAA flight out. Here we were blessed to enjoyed two months before, due to business demands, he had to repatriate on the last first flight out.

The twist in the tale is that he had just arrived home, when I headed out the door for my first exploratory meeting with the Ladles of Love Sandwich Drive team and my life in service kicked in – I responded to a plea for help and every fiber of my body joined the call for action to feed the starving and destitute people of the Western Cape.

From that minute on I never experienced one day of lockdown as I worked 24/7 as Campaign Director for Ladles of Love driving fundraising and landed up finding homes like CTICC and Grand West for our feeding scheme expansion.

On the 5th June my lockdown began with isolation – I found out, through a self-elected test, I was Covid-Positive.

Lessons Learnt

The Coronavirus hits you where you are most vulnerable and invades your body until at some point you think: "What the heaven's name is going on". You feel out of sorts and strange – super, super emotional and stressed out. I might suffer from genetic chronic hypertension, but the truth is I am bullet proof, I am a veteran at dealing with highly stressful situations, having been in the large event business forever! But I had become a victim of anxiety attacks with my blood pressure spiking giving rise to a beating lump in my neck – almost like an extra heart!

I had no clue this was my experience of Coronavirus – this realisation came in isolation because I finally had time to just be. Be with myself only after a hundred people daily at the CTICC. I spent time and had a meeting with myself to figure out what on earth was going on in my body and realised that I had been sick way and before the 5th June, more like 5th May.

The symptoms I had did not tick a symptomatic Covid-19 case but after much reading up and research aided by a Facebook page, Survivor Corps, I learnt my experience was in fact something shared by other victims. The big learning was – you might at some point be contagious and that is scary, but mostly by the time you take a test, you are past it like me. What adds insult to injury is the recovery period can take up to six months and counting – as no-one really knows.

The truth is you cannot get re-infected for the simple reason as you are still infected and experiencing on going symptoms that you have learned to recognise. Your life is changed and you will never think the same again. Why? You dodged a lethal bullet and are simply a statistic of infected, not recovered and but thankfully not dead. Millions are not going to be that fortunate and I will live my new life in gratitude.

Elderly Rebel

My Covid-19 story is one of being bamboozled, with my worst nightmares and wildest dreams realised, simultaneously. How is it possible to be terrified, exhausted and exhilarated simultaneously? Every day during lockdown I would wake up, jump up and could not wait to drive to a city that was fast asleep to connect with my newfound colleagues.

These are super, smart people who every day continue to enrich my knowledge – they have become my Covid-19 family and new besties! We work side by side united in our passion and purpose, determined to feed as many of our destitute people meals daily.

I feel proud to be walking my 'ubuntu' talk and finally using my years of creative, critical and strategic thinking, to help incredible community leaders with courage and huge hearts, find sustainable ways to feed their communities.

New Skills

I have engaged with stakeholders I never imagined would consider taking my calls – from national government to local our local premier, CEOs to famous celebrities, multi-national marketing directors to head of faculties at University – all on a quest to open doors and opportunities for Ladles of Love to meet the growing demands of their beneficiaries.

The big-time bonus is I have accelerated by understanding of the internet of things and can work remotely using sophisticated technology that was previously way and beyond my comprehension.

The Way Forward

The phrase "I can't", anyone who has worked for me will tell you is not in my dictionary.

Then for good measure, add a humanitarian crisis like Covid-19 into the mix and suddenly I have developed the ability to ask for help from anyone however high up a ladder and supposedly untouchable. I now have the courage to speak out and dream bigger than I ever imagined possible and succeed.

I have finally found my voice. I can just be me. I am no longer trying to do anything at all except for being authentic, passionate and determined to meet my goals because they just suddenly feel right.

Why? I am on a purpose-led journey, in a cycle of continuous learning and on a mission to make a difference by creating jobs and economic opportunities for the youth of our county, one person at a time.

What of Rainbow? We are re-birthing Rainbow as a purpose driven, integrated cause marketing agency with the sole goal of connecting brands and NPOs and in so doing, forming symbiotic partnerships.

As a collective of human activists, we will be catalysts of change – humanising business and advising non-profits with a view to driving social innovation.

Message of Hope

"Harness hope by trusting in the process of life. Try not to figure out your destination, as it is the journey that matters, punctuated with continuous learning and being open to opportunities that show up by connecting with smarter people than you."

Connect with Ali here https://www.facebook.com/AliMacMentoring/

Chapter 7

Wisdom

MAKE A DIFFERENCE

Featuring:

- Kim Whitaker: Ubuntu Beds

- Guy Cluver: Bellevue Cafe

- Cindy Norcott: Robin Hood Foundation

"Knowing others is wisdom, knowing yourself is enlightenment."
– *Lao Tzu*

UBUNTU
by Kim Whitaker

About Kim

> *A zealous mother and entrepreneur living and working in South Africa, Kim is passionate about youth tourism, education and entrepreneurship. Kim is the founder of Ubuntu Beds, co-founder of Once Travel and Youth Tourism Academy in Khwela, and an EO Cape Town member. For fun, she nurtures her vegetable garden in Tulbagh, and, since lockdown, has pretended to homeschool her kids, Julia and Leo. Her happy place is being knee-deep in powder snow somewhere off-piste.*

Slippery Slopes

In early March 2020, I was so excited to travel to Germany, where I was going to talk at a travel conference in Berlin. But by the time I landed, I learnt that members of the German team hosting the conference had contracted Covid-19 and that the conference had been cancelled.

Nevertheless, I made the most of my time in the city and, despite the rising numbers of Covid-19 cases (from 150 to 2,200 in the week I was there), continued on a much-awaited skiing weekend to Austria where I had spent many ski seasons as an instructor in my 20s. I rationalised the trip by saying to myself, "Corona is just the flu, I'll be fine!"

While we enjoyed our time in the sun and snow, the health and economic repercussions of Covid-19 escalated quickly; things became tense and alarming in a very short space of time. By the end of the 10 days I was in Europe, Italy (a mere 100km from where we had been skiing) had closed its borders and southern Germany's case numbers had sky rocketed. Tourism came to a grinding halt, and I watched as the businesses of many of my friends and colleagues in Europe dwindled. Within just a few short days, mass retrenchments were taking place.

It won't Happen to me

Back in South Africa, I went to collect my children from school and, while waiting for them, received a message informing me that if I had been travelling in Europe I would need to go into self-quarantine. Initially, I was furious. I felt this precaution was unfair and unnecessary, and an infringement on my freedom.

The next day, in an effort to "prove them wrong", I was tested for Covid-19, and two days later my results came back positive. It was a shock to realise that I had contracted the virus, and to consider what the repercussions of this diagnosis were for my two small children and husband.

I made a list of all the people I had come into contact with and called every one, handing them over to the National Institute of Communicable Diseases to be monitored. I called the mother of the children I had lifted home that first day and my entire office staff, all of whom had to go into 14 days of precautionary self-quarantine. The school that my children attend was shut down because I had been on the premises.

Overnight, our home turned into a hospital: we cleaned and disinfected everything. Everyone had their own cutlery, crockery and glasses. We slept in separate bedrooms and became very conscious of eating healthily. I took vitamins, drank a lot of water, and made a deliberate effort to keep calm and exercise regularly.

The Impact on Tourism

During this time, I also realised that my tourism business was destined for disaster. As tourists flocked home, our two hotels — Once in Cape Town and Once in Joburg — went from 96% occupancy on Tuesday to 60% on Wednesday. By Friday, they were empty. Within a week, the tourists had gone and our business was flailing.

It was clear that our industry was on the front line and that we would be one of the first to feel the economic impact of the virus. On 15 March, I remember listening to Dr Jacob Zwaan, a fellow Entrepreneurs' Organization (EO) member, telling us about his small Italian town of Lombardy, which was at the epicentre of the virus and was experiencing 400 to 800 deaths a day. He said Italy was in the midst of a medical crisis that was dwarfing the economic crisis. "We should have used empty hotels to safely accommodate medical workers near their jobs," he said.

In Italy, these valuable workers were forced to travel home after a long day amid restrictions on public transport. They also ran the risk of exposing their own families to the virus. Often, they ended up sleeping in their cars in an effort to keep their loved ones safe. Dr Zwaan's comment was a light bulb moment for me. Both my parents are doctors – I knew I had to do something.

Hotel Rooms for Healthcare Workers

I went to my team and we came up with a plan. We realised that hospital managers were facing many challenges, one of which was not being able to see to the after-hours needs of their staff, and that's where we could help.

We decided to make our hotel rooms available to healthcare workers for free and to look for money for the running costs, either from donations or through funding from key role players. We offered medical personnel accommodation in both of our two hotels, each of which has 50 rooms, and within a month, had created a logo, designed a website and built a platform. Ubuntu Beds was born.

The Spirit of Ubuntu

"Ubuntu" is a Nguni word that means "humanity towards others". It describes the sense that "I am because we are" and involves looking after those in need because we understand they are part of the fabric that holds our community together.

As awareness of our project grew, others in the tourism industry wanted to help, and started to offer their accommodation on our platform, too. As at the middle of June 2020, 1,100 businesses had jumped on board and 480 individual healthcare workers had made applications. Some of these applications were urgent (for Covid-19 cases who were unable to self-isolate, for example) and others were backup plans in case things got worse.

Over 17,000 rooms are now available across the country and we are the preferred partners to Mediclinic, Life Healthcare and a number of public hospitals. We have housed over 200 healthcare workers around South Africa in bed and breakfasts, guesthouses, hotels and apartments for anywhere between a week and a month, and our moonshot goal is to host 2,500 healthcare workers during the course of the pandemic.

The Power of a Network

In South Africa, infections have started to rise dramatically, and I'm grateful that we had the time to map out a plan. There are 600 hospitals around South Africa, and coordinating this effort has been a mammoth task that would not have been possible without the many volunteers and small businesses who jumped on board to help, many of whom were connected through the country's EO network.

These include Ross Drakes and the team from Nicework (EO Johannesburg) who jumped at the chance to get involved and have gone above and beyond in designing our beautiful logo, website and social media channels. Legalese (also in the EO family) is doing all the legal work, and the team from Esri built the platform we're using to geocode the accommodation options closest to hospitals. The reservations team is made up almost entirely of volunteers who lost their jobs in tourism as a result of Covid-19, and FirstRand's SPIRE Fund has funded our operational costs and paid for the vital post-stay decontamination fees.

In one project, corporates, entrepreneurs and volunteers have come together to make a difference, and to help the healthcare workers who may be at your side, or the side of someone you love, during this time.

It is my belief that human beings are exceptionally resilient. I've been surprised that I'm not grieving for my dying business, but that instead, I'm excited by the challenges of solving a new problem. I have learnt that I thrive in uncertainty, and have loved how alive I have felt in the last few months as I navigate the crisis day by day. It's clear to me that we're all in this together, and that we truly are doing this work in the spirit of ubuntu. I am because we are.

Message of Hope

"We're all in this together."

Connect with us here https://www.ubuntubeds.org

A HUMBLING EXPERIENCE
by Guy Cluver

About Guy

> Guy has been in the restaurant business since he worked at the famous Legends restaurant in Musgrave as a waiter in 1990. Since then, he has run numerous Keg-affiliated restaurants around South Africa, and has owned the Stocker's Arms in Kloof and the News Cafe in Musgrave.
>
> After selling the latter two restaurants and opening Butcher Boys and Franki Bananaz in Hillcrest in 2004, Guy went on to open Bellevue Cafe on 1 August 2010 with his business partner, Chris Black. In 2013, Guy and Chris founded the Lupa Osteria restaurant group, a share of which was sold to Famous Brands in 2013. Today, there are 13 Lupa restaurants across the country.
>
> Guy is married to his childhood sweetheart, Shelley, and has two daughters, Sarah and Amy. His passions are wine, coffee, pizza, friendship and endurance sports.

A Family

I opened Bellevue Cafe in 2010 and most of the staff have been with me from the start. We are part of the community, we're a family, and our restaurant is like my second home. When lockdown hit, my priority was my staff. While we managed to keep most of them going through UIF contributions, my 16 waiters were a source of concern as they survive on tips.

After a week of lockdown, my younger daughter, Amy, suggested that we distribute meal vouchers. We started selling vouches, with 50% of the value going to our waiters and 50% to cover VAT and the cost of sale when the voucher is redeemed. Our community was incredibly generous and R100,000 was donated in just 10 days. This helped us to keep our waitering staff fed and safe at home, but the long-term problem of looking after them until we were allowed to reopen was still an issue.

A Turning Point

On 4 May, a friend, Julika Falconer, sent me a video clip that I ignored, thinking it was just another restaurant loan scheme. Later that day, she contacted me again and urged me to watch it. I'm so glad I did. The video featured a restaurant called the Beerhouse in Cape Town that had started a soup kitchen from their restaurant. The owner had realised that people weren't being fed during the crisis and decided to do something about it.

The video made me realise that there was no reason why we couldn't use our beautiful restaurant as a soup kitchen. We quickly got to work. We employed our waiters to do the cooking, and set up a rotating roster in which five waiters, usually from the same family, work every third day.

The Kindness of Strangers

Social media has been amazing, especially Facebook, which we have been using to send out our appeals. We need R15,000 a week to keep the project going. Just the other day, we received an anonymous donation of R60,000, and subsequently over R150,000 in further donations. Gestures like this make me feel quite emotional. Once people realise where their money is going, their support is overwhelming. Our community knows that what they give us goes to the right place.

We've partnered with Julika's NGO, Zero2Five, and all the donations are running through their bank account, which is being independently audited.

To date, I have only bought 10 litres of cooking oil; all the other ingredients have been donated. Every morning people arrive with bakkie loads of food, including cabbages lettuce and kale, and local supermarkets are now making donations, too. It has truly been remarkable. RCL foods, which supplies chicken to KFC, contacted us because they didn't have capacity to store some of their chicken. Soon after, two tonnes of chicken arrived, which we have been using to make a hearty stew that we serve with rice. The meals are chilled overnight and distributed to local communities the following day. As of the end of May, we had served more than 130,000 meals, and our target is 250,000 meals by the end of June.

Humbling Deliveries

Just 400 meters from our beautiful home on a golf estate are communities of people who have nothing. Many of these people are Zimbabweans and Malawians who don't qualify for government grants in South Africa. From Monday to Friday, we pack 100 five-litre buckets of food that get collected and delivered to these communities. My wife and I do the Friday deliveries and the experience has been profoundly moving.

It's been uplifting and inspiring to be part of this. It has changed our relationship with our staff and our standing within our community. The challenge is going to be to keep this going once lockdown ends. The need is dreadful; it's clear to us that many more people will die of starvation than of Covid-19.

I recently read an article in the Wall Street Journal about restaurants in Paris and London that remained open during World War II despite the circumstances. It is wonderful to think that, in our own way, we are performing a similar function. We are helping people – helping them to get through this difficult time and to receive the food they so desperately need.

A Reawakening of Empathy

Before, our business was all about profit. The Covid-19 crisis has been humbling – we've lost a lot of money, but at the same time, we've done something meaningful.

This experience has forced me to become more community conscious. It has reawakened the empathy I used to have as a youngster. I would never have driven my bakkie to deliver food to Embo Valley before. Just two months ago, I would have told myself that I had too much else going on. I feel I have gained tremendous insight into the lives of my staff, where they live and the struggles they face.

I also realise we can't go back to the way we operated before. The long-term sustainability of our business is critical. It has been an incredibly hard year so far, and anyone who breaks even would have done very well. We can't bleed out. We have to make sure we have a business when this is all over.

Message of Hope

"For now, I know that I would rather be losing money and making a difference than losing money and sitting at home."

Connect with us here www.bellevuecafe.co.za

HEART FOR PEOPLE
by Cindy Norcott

About Cindy

> *Over the past 26 years, Cindy has honed her skills as a sought-after motivational speaker, business trainer, business coach and mentor, best-selling author and award-winning charity head. This she has achieved while still running her Westville-based recruitment agencies, Pro Appointments and Pro Talent, which have won more than 20 awards for business excellence over the years. Cindy is the author of the best-selling business book, How to be Unstoppable, and has won many awards for her entrepreneurial endeavours, including the BWA Regional Achiever of the Year award.*
>
> *In 2005, Cindy started the Robin Hood Foundation, an NGO to which she donates her time in her capacity as chairperson. The Robin Hood Foundation runs more than 120 charitable outreach projects every year around KwaZulu-Natal, making a difference to the lives of the poorest members of society. For her involvement in this work, Cindy has been awarded a Paul Harris award from Westville Rotary and, in 2016; she was awarded the Sunday Tribune Lead SA KZN Hero of the Year award.*

People over Profit

In March 2020, lockdown was imminent and people everywhere were discussing ways to save their businesses. A number of strategies were being considered, including retrenching staff, cutting salaries, and finding ways to scale down by putting profit first. Although some of these ideas make practical business sense, as someone with a passion for people I simply couldn't buy into them.

For years I have followed my intuition and it's been my greatest asset. I knew that, just because we were starting to go through a difficult time, I couldn't let my staff at my recruitment agencies down. And so I decided to keep my entire team on their full salaries and to stay true to our core business values: communicating as much as possible and staying positive.

I have spent years building a great brand and a strong team, and I knew that, now more than ever, I had to be a leader.

Networking and Growth

We started by focusing on what we could control, like building our network. We were under no illusions that initially it would feel like we were wading through wet cement – and indeed our first 60-day sprint felt like a 60-day slog – but we knew that, as time passed, things would get easier.

We have tried to work towards micro goals every day. We are constantly looking for ways to add value to our clients so that we can be seen as caring market leaders. We have taught our candidates to use Zoom and have shared COVID-19 policies and documents with our clients. Our business has evolved from a sales-driven environment to one that concentrates on networking and growth.

I've also been offering free motivational webinars for our clients, and have been sharing inspirational content on our digital platforms. Although this aspect of the work has been exhausting at times, the incredible feedback we've received has made it all worthwhile.

The Robin Hood Foundation

The Robin Hood Foundation started in 2005 as a small project, collecting and distributing baby clothes to underprivileged families. In 2020, our plan was to build three crèches. The foundation has only one permanent staff member and the rest of the team are volunteers between 55 and 83 years old. As COVID-19 threatens the older generation in particular, we decided to send our volunteers home.

On the Saturday before lockdown I went shopping for my family and bought enough food to last us 12 days. When I saw an avocado seller at the traffic lights, I realised that this was not the time to build crèches – you can't eat a crèche. No, this was the time to shift our strategy and focus on feeding people. The foundation quickly went into high alert and we started to look into how we could supply food to those in need.

Rallying to Help the Hungry

At the start of lockdown, the foundation had approximately R500,000 in its bank account, money that we decided to use buy and distribute food to various communities. Through my connections in the Entrepreneurs' Organization, I heard about farmers who ordinarily supply food to restaurants and hotels, and who were now looking for other channels to distribute their produce. We connected with these farmers and they supplied us with gems squashes, potatoes and mielies.

We also spoke to a dairy with which we have worked before. They are an essential service and have big trucks, and so we started to collaborate with them to distribute masks, maize and milk. As we drew on these networks, different businesses began contacting us to offer goods — from sanitiser and baby products to bakkie loads of avocados and financial aid. Our 15 years' worth of work with community members and local businesses has stood us in good stead.

Robin Hood is a God-given project and people appreciate our humility and transparency. Our big hairy audacious goal was to raise R1 million in May. We pursued many different avenues, and ultimately raised over R3.5 million in cash and food donations.

I believe we haven't seen the full impact of this crisis yet and that the need for help is likely to continue. And there is the concern that people's kindness will only extend up to a point and then even more desperate people will be in trouble. If I go onto our Facebook page and read some of the messages, it's heartbreaking. I think we are going to be mopping up the pieces for a long time.

Living on Faith

Years ago in a group that I belonged to, I remember a particular discussion about missionaries who live on faith alone. I've been thinking a lot about this, especially given that there is so little trustworthy information available at the moment. Currently, it feels like we're all living on faith.

What has struck me the most is how generous people are, even when they have lost everything. A friend of mine lost her job and still insisted on giving us money. The generosity of people has been a humbling experience for me.

I have faith, but I believe have put too much of it into my business. As a result, I've taken a real emotional knock during this time because we're not achieving what we would ordinarily. I've had to learn from people: like the man selling avocados who, standing there smiling and living on faith. Through this crisis, I feel I am truly beginning to understand faith and abundance.

Slow Down and Simplify

My biggest lesson has been to slow down. I feel like I've been rushing my whole life. This period has taught me to look at my basket of responsibilities and clear out what's no longer needed. The season for some things is over. Now is the time to simplify, be humble and ask for help. I'm not used to asking for help so being bold is another lesson I have had to learn.

I have to talk to myself to stop myself being anxious and stressed about my business and the foundation. Things will improve, we have a great brand a massive database of people who love our project. And if the government won't help the people, we will help the people. Although this experience has taken its toll on every aspect of my life, I know that now is the time to lead.

Message of Hope

"Be Resilient, Stay Connected."

Connect with us here www.robinhoodfoundation.co.za

INDEX

www.ingramcontent.com/pod-product-compliance
Lightning Source LLC
Chambersburg PA
CBHW070925270326
41927CB00011B/2726